238.7

BUSINESS OWNERS WHO ARE
BLIND OR VISUALLY IMPAIRED

JOBS THAT MATTER

An engaging series written by Deborah Kendrick and devoted to the personal stories of individuals who are blind or visually impaired and who are successful in fields of work they have chosen, *Jobs That Matter* profiles inspiring role models for blind and visually impaired students who want to achieve satisfaction in the world of work.

TITLES IN THE JOBS THAT MATTER SERIES

Teachers Who Are Blind or Visually Impaired

ALSO AVAILABLE FROM AFB PRESS

Jobs To Be Proud Of: Profiles of Workers Who Are Blind or Visually Impaired
Career Perspectives: Interviews with Blind and Visually Impaired Professionals

JOBS THAT MATTER

Business Owners Who Are Blind or Visually Impaired

Deborah Kendrick

PRESS

New York

Library of Congress Cataloging-in-Publication Data

Kendrick, Deborah, 1950–
    Business owners who are blind or visually impaired / Deborah Kendrick.
    p. cm -- (Jobs that matter)
    ISBN 0-89128-324-2 (alk. paper)
    1. Blind businesspeople--United States--Biography. 2. Visually handicapped businesspeople--United States--Biography. I. Title.
    HV1792.A3 K45 2000
    338.7'092'273--dc21
    [B]   00-057591

The American Foundation for the Blind—the organization to which Helen Keller devoted more than 40 years of her life—is a national nonprofit whose mission is to eliminate the inequities faced by the 10 million Americans who are blind or visually impaired. Headquartered in New York City, AFB maintains offices in Atlanta, Chicago, Dallas, San Francisco, and a governmental relations office in Washington, DC.

It is the policy of the American Foundation for the Blind to use in the first printing of its books acid-free paper that meets the ANSI Z39.48 Standard. The infinity symbol that appears above indicates that the paper in this printing meets that standard.

CONTENTS

FOREWORD

BEING AN ENTREPRENEUR seems almost a genetic affair. One child will set up a lemonade stand or pet-sitting enterprise with the boldness of the Wright Brothers taking flight, while another would prefer being offered a job.

What, then, are the skills required of adults establishing businesses of their own? Self-confidence, certainly. High motivation, definitely. And perhaps a higher-than-average share of impetuous thrill-seeking and a willingness to crash, burn, and start all over again.

When we add blindness or visual impairment to the mix, the stakes are higher still and courage indisputable. The people profiled in this book are, without doubt, steel-willed, self-disciplined human beings who believe in themselves and their own abilities to succeed and who are sufficiently intrepid to risk finance and future for the realization of a dream.

Deborah Kendrick brings these 16 business owners to life in a way that enables us to see the improbable as possible, and to aspire to shaping other dreams. Through their stories, we witness how each addressed the challenges posed by blindness and incorporated the necessary techniques into a formula for success. The pragmatics of business plans, inventory, and bookkeeping face every brave new business owner, with or without sight. The people in this book, however, have confronted the additional challenges of accessing print information, maintaining control in visual environments, and providing leadership to those who are sometimes readers or guides. Through their engaging tales of success, we learn that it can be done: a blind or visually impaired person can build, operate, and thrive in a business that is matched to his or her talents. As we come to know them, we get a clearer picture of how they did it—and learn how we can, too.

Ben Cohen and Jerry Greenfield
Co-founders of Ben & Jerry's

Ben Cohen and Jerry Greenfield founded Ben & Jerry's, Vermont's Finest Ice Cream and Frozen Yogurt, in 1978 in a renovated gas station in Burlington, Vermont.

INTRODUCTION

HARD WORK, determination, belief in oneself: These ingredients for success are as American as blue jeans and as venerable as the wisdom of Benjamin Franklin. They are also at the core of the stories told again and again, with various themes, by the people who are profiled in this book.

Traci Parks, a visually impaired architectural photographer, likes to quote her grandfather's saying that "Yes, a millionaire is someone who is very lucky. And the harder he works, the luckier he gets." Although none of the people you will meet in this book is yet a millionaire, they are all extremely successful and, as diverse as their chosen professions are, they have all shown strong determination in the number of hours and years they have been willing to commit to realize their dreams.

From cabinetmaker to deal maker, from New York to California, the people in this book have many things in common: high energy, experiences of near disaster, determination, a strong belief in themselves, and an honest assessment of blindness.

"You have to be parsimonious with your time" is the way Larry Chase, an entrepreneur and author who saw the economic power of the World Wide

Web long before many of his sighted contemporaries, puts it. Chase's belief is rooted both in the maxim that "Time is money" and in his admission that limited vision dictates a need for greater time and focus to accomplish most tasks.

"I have to take into account that it takes me three to four times longer to do some things as it does a sighted person," confirms business owner Richard Oehm. Kevin Kelley considers the recognition of that limitation an asset, advising would-be entrepreneurs to "surround yourself with people whose limitations and abilities complement your own." Similarly, Lou Fioritto made the one thing he knew better than any sighted person because of his blindness (how best to present braille as a form of usable literacy in the marketplace) the touchstone for launching his triumphant business venture.

Intrinsic faith in a higher power is another recurring theme that appears in the accounts of building companies and achieving success. "My relationship with God cannot be overlooked," reflects Steve Hanamura when considering an explanation for his success. This theme is echoed in the accounts of several other people you will meet in these pages and is perhaps best summed up by Parks when she says, "Coincidence is God's way of remaining anonymous."

There were other striking similarities among the people who are profiled here. They all actively pursued whatever adaptive tools and techniques were necessary to accomplish the work they wanted to do. Twelve of the 16 use braille to some extent or exclusively as their means of maintaining records and gaining access to information. The four who are not braille users are able to use print with magnification effectively. In many cases, the kind of business an individual established evolved from a specific interest or talent. And, finally, each of them radiates high self-esteem, an unabashed zeal for self-promotion, and a penchant for taking risks.

As something of an entrepreneur myself, building a business of freelance writing and public speaking since 1981, I was both inspired and humbled when I conducted the interviews for this book. Having persistence and focus, setting priorities, establishing plans and living by them, seeking the 51st way to solve a problem when the first 50 have failed—these are the lessons I learned. Having said that, Nick Medina's advice is sage as well: "If the first thing you try doesn't succeed, try something else."

All the people in this book are visually impaired, yet they have remarkable vision, insight, and foresight. Read their stories and learn. Whether you plan to set up a business like one of those described here or do something entirely different, listen to Chase when he says, "You might as well be passionate about what you choose to do because you're going to spend so much of your time doing it."

—Deborah Kendrick

BUSINESS OWNERS WHO ARE BLIND OR VISUALLY IMPAIRED

ABOUT BARRY S. SCHEUR

BUSINESS
Scheur Management Group

LOCATION
Newton, Massachusetts

AGE
48

CAUSE OF VISUAL IMPAIRMENT
Retrolental fibroplasia at birth

VISUAL ACUITY
Total blindness

MANAGED CARE CONSULTANT
Barry S. Scheur

"Business depends upon the art of communicating and getting along with people and in making a difference in people's lives."

B ARRY SCHEUR GRADUATED from Yale University in 1976 in the top 10 percent of his law school class. Yet, while his friends were offered jobs in prestigious law firms around the country, he received close to 300 letters of rejection. Today, given his success, some of those companies might reconsider their hasty assessment of what a blind person can do.

"I became a lawyer because it was the only thing I knew a blind person could do," Scheur explains. As a teenager, he started to read the *Braille Forum,* and from that reading began to correspond with the blind lawyer who founded the American Blind Lawyers Association.

After a stint as a lawyer with an Atlanta law firm, Scheur was offered a position as general counsel at a fledgling health maintenance organization (HMO) that evolved into the Eastern Region of Kaiser Permanente, one of the oldest and most prestigious health plans in the country. Since he had worked with the HMO on keeping health care coverage for the firm's employees, his name came to mind when the HMO wanted to hire a lawyer.

In 1982, after having been promoted to the position of chief operating officer, he left the HMO to become the president of a start-up HMO and returned to Boston, where had received his bachelor's degree from Tufts University 10 years before. "I got fired from that job a year later, mostly because I was working in a city government and didn't understand politics or how to manage people very well," he recalls.

Scheur started his own consulting practice out of his home, and two years later, he established a relationship with the first of two law firms that lasted 3½ years. "By the end of 1988, I had enough of law practice and had built a considerable managed-care consulting business as a subsidiary of the law firm. Clients were seeking my business advice more often than my legal advice, and I decided to build my own company with the people I developed. That was the origin of Scheur Management."

Since 1988, the consulting practice has been extremely successful, both from a relationship-building and a business perspective. Scheur counts among his friends political leaders and medical, corporate, and educational policy-makers around the country and among his successes the turnaround of Blue Cross/Blue Shield of Rhode Island and the creation or turnaround of major HMOs in Florida, Kentucky, Ohio, and Oklahoma.

Today, Scheur Management Group is a $7 million company with 25 employees and business in

44 states. To diversify from consulting, Scheur also created a venture-capital arm that makes start-up investments in health care services and technology and an HMO-acquisition company that buys and runs troubled health plans. Colleagues describe Scheur as dynamic, unconventional, and tireless. His workdays are long, and he is constantly generating new ideas.

"I often begin work at five or six in the morning," Scheur explains, "and I hire people who can keep the same hours. Many of my key management executives, four women in particular, are used to me calling at 5 A.M. with an idea or a request for a document or information I need to see that day—and that's the way they like to work, too."

Scheur has served as the president of six HMOs and has consulted with hundreds of organizations that are affected by or involved with managed care: from fledgling integrated delivery systems to Fortune 500 corporations, medical societies, state and federal regulatory agencies, and health care reform groups. The primary business of his firm is to advise, build, manage, or rescue companies in the managed care industry, and this fast-talking, pipe-smoking maverick accomplishes that work with a speed and alacrity that novice onlookers may miss by blinking.

The only consistent factor in Scheur's workday may well be that he never seems to stop. Two to three days a week, he flies to various places in the country to meet with boards of directors or senior executives, make presentations, or solve difficult operational or organizational challenges. If you see him in his Newton, Massachusetts, office, where he tends to spend one or two days a week, it may seem as though he is not doing much at all. Most of the time, he is either talking on the phone or typing on one of his braille computers. Otherwise his desk is clear—except for the few dozen pipes, one of which he is frequently puffing on while thinking, writing, and making plans.

"I'm primarily a deal maker, an advice giver, and a problem solver," Scheur says. "I'm in the business of making deals, introducing people, and creating opportunities where the whole is greater than the sum of the parts. . . . The art of communicating ideas passionately and getting along with people—those are the skills that make my company a success."

So what are the deals and problems Scheur fixes? Some days, he advises such companies as Procter & Gamble and Hershey Foods on restructuring their health care benefits. Other days, he oversees an HMO in financial trouble at the mandate of a state insurance department. He may run an organizationally dysfunctional hospital system to straighten out its business, rescue an HMO by deploying a group of his experienced senior executives, or work with physicians to negotiate effective health care contracts with intractable insurers.

Sometimes, his staff may provide the leadership for a start-up company with tight deadlines and budgetary pressures. Sometimes, Scheur may restructure a company's finances or obtain venture capital for a promising new business.

Braille literacy is the centerpiece of his brilliant management of the ebb and flow of incessant information. Scheur writes drafts of all documents—proposals, letters, and presentations—in braille and then forwards them to his secretary for polishing and eliminating what he and his secretary affectionately dub his "braillos." There are four scanners in his office, and his office support staff of six has scanned countless pages for uploading for Scheur's use and review.

Scheur has a variety of braille computers—among them two versions of braille laptops—the DOS-based David from TeleSensory Corporation and SuperBraille from Advanced Access Devices. However, his communication device of choice is the 40-cell Braille Lite, a sophisticated, lightweight notetaker from Blazie Engineering, which handles voluminous amounts of reading, writing, and E-mail exchanges daily. On the Braille Lite, he makes notes from his numerous phone conversations, board meetings, and conference calls; drafts proposals; and reads the endless stream of information that he downloads for reading at another time.

His secretary has become expert at interpreting, formatting, and uploading all types of documents, spreadsheets, and graphs that she sends electronically to her boss in braille; she also back-translates into print proposals and other documents that he has written to present to clients.

Scheur estimates that 70 percent of his time in the office is spent on the phone. Much of his travel time (which he estimates at about 200 days a year) is also spent talking on either a hotel phone or the mobile phone that he always takes with him.

Scheur delegates many routine tasks to others: editing and formatting documents he has written, managing the administrative operations of the company, keeping track of financial records, and accounting.

"I have no idea how to type or read a spreadsheet," he explains. "I know, however, when one of my staff reads a financial statement to me how to interpret it, and I can pull from a spreadsheet the facts I need to make decisions that keep companies in business."

Blind since birth, Scheur credits the way he was raised with much of his nonstop confidence in his own abilities. He went to public schools with sighted children, went to summer camp with his sighted brother, learned to waterski and to play everything from football to chess and the piano.

He also learned at an early age that he could lead and motivate people, and it was that confidence in himself that drove him to begin his own company. Being in business for himself has led to tremendous success, but there have been troubled times as well. "I once had to ask my senior executives to take a 30 percent pay cut when we lost a major client in 1991. We almost went broke, but I was able to replace the lost consulting business and pay back the reductions plus a bonus for the faith the staff showed in me," he recalls.

Scheur is candid in pointing out the potential pitfalls for a blind business owner. Once, when he was less cautious, an employee took advantage of his blindness by using a corporate credit card to finance part of her wedding. Now he has a trusted comptroller and treasurer who monitor accounts carefully, and feels confident that such an incident will not happen again. In addition, 14 of his 25 employees are senior consultants, who are responsible for making decisions that involve millions of dollars. Building trust among his employees and his clients is key to both the success of the company and his personal competence, he says.

Even after Scheur was abused by some clients and sued by some former disgruntled employees, he still believes in taking risks and in using his instincts to hire talented people who may be rejected elsewhere. "Three quarters of our senior executives are women, and I think they do a better job than men most of the time when given unique challenges beyond what they thought their capabilities to be," he says.

Still, he notes, there is an art to finding the right balance in dealing with employees who work closely with a blind boss. "When I'm traveling with my staff, I use a cane and am always following somebody around. They may need to read something to me on site, grab my coffee, or otherwise give some personal assistance. In other words, I sometimes have a level of dependence on them that a sighted executive wouldn't have. It's harder to criticize when you're dependent on people. [There's] an important balance, however, [between supervising people and sometimes being dependent upon them for assistance] that has to be maintained."

It seems to be a balance he maintains with panache. His staff not only work for him, but *with* him every step of the way and show their loyalty and affection easily. Each year, for example, as a holiday tribute to Scheur, his staff underwrites and dedicates the brailling of one title by National Braille Press in his honor.

When traveling alone to other cities, Scheur uses credit cards for almost everything. His company contracts with a number of taxi and limousine companies, so that his time is used effectively and cash is rarely necessary.

His memory is extraordinary, as is his grasp of financial and business concepts. Yet, he is as much in the business of human relations as in the world of finance. He makes friends easily and builds trust charismatically. "When we're taking over and running a company, there are so many questions to address. What do we do with these people? How do we rebuild morale, take on competitors, increase the business's profitability, and instill confidence in customers and business partners? To make it all work, I need to be skilled in solving problems, human relations, communication, getting people to work with one another."

Above all else, Scheur believes that "business depends upon the art of communicating and getting along with people and in making a difference in people's lives." He has done both with sheer brilliance.

THREE TIPS FOR SUCCESS
1. Learn to use braille.
2. Never believe you cannot do something. There is always a way to try almost anything.
3. Concentrate on writing well as a form of communication. The art of communication—getting along with people and writing clearly—is essential.

ADAPTIVE EQUIPMENT: A 40-cell Braille Lite by Blazie Engineering; a 386 DOS-based David laptop with braille display by TeleSensory Corporation; a Pentium II SuperBraille laptop with braille display by Advanced Access Devices; scanners for feeding print to computers for braille translation; Megadots by Duxbury Systems and QuickBraille braille-translation software packages; and a variety of audiotape recorders that are capable of playing four-track Talking Book-style recordings. (See the Resources section at the end of this book for more information about this equipment.)

SALARY: The year-end success of the company has a direct impact on Scheur's salary. In 1999 Scheur's estimated salary was $600,000.

ABOUT TRACI PARKS

BUSINESS
Miracle Images

LOCATION
Columbus, Ohio

AGE
32

CAUSE OF VISUAL IMPAIRMENT
Degenerative myopia

VISUAL ACUITY
20/400 (60/120, its metric equivalent)

ARCHITECTURAL PHOTOGRAPHER

Traci Parks

*"You have to follow up every lead,
make every possible contact.
It's up to me to make those calls,
do the research, go after the business."*

IN 1989, TRACI PARKS THOUGHT she had her life lined up exactly the way she wanted it: She had graduated with a bachelor's degree in communication management from the University of Dayton and had landed her dream job. The position, coordinator of public relations at a Catholic high school in Cincinnati, similar to the school she had attended in Hamilton, Ohio, turned out to be other than the dream job she had imagined.

Measured in public relations terms, Parks did well on the job—recruiting students and getting the school on network television and in a variety of print publications—but budgets were tight, and the indoor nine-to-five life was not for her. Two years into the job, she was being treated for clinical depression.

Soon after her release from the hospital, she bought a camera. There was no logic in the purchase,

Parks recalls. She had never taken pictures or even had a desire to take pictures.

"I was broke, and I was buying a $350 camera," she laughs now. She says more seriously that what we call "coincidence" is merely "God's way of remaining anonymous."

The first picture Parks took, a field of tulips, was selected out of more than 1,000 entries to appear in an annual collection called *The Best of College Photography.* That success and the elimination of her public relations position led her to a new vocation: architectural photography.

When Parks was five years old, her ophthalmologist diagnosed her "nearsightedness" as degenerative myopia, warning her family that her vision would probably diminish over time. Still, by holding books close to her eyes and always sitting in the front row of the classroom, she managed to get through school with honors and without adaptations.

When she enrolled in the Ohio Institute of Photography in December 1992, she already knew that she needed sharp edges in images to make good pictures. In other words, she knew that photographing buildings and products worked well for her and that she would never be a fashion or portrait photographer because there are too many soft lines in the human form for Parks to see through a camera lens. Her only adaptation during two years of photography school was substituting another course for the required course in editorial photography (photojournalism), in which the goal was to locate human subjects, photograph them, and print the photographs in a four-hour period. Parks could not physically focus on people well enough to do the assignment and was allowed to replace the course with an internship in architectural photography. "I fell in love with shooting buildings," she says, "the exteriors, the interiors—I just loved it."

Three months after she received her diploma from the Ohio Institute of Photography, Parks was driving to the home of a photographer friend when something suddenly blurred her vision; she had experienced severe hemorrhages in both eyes. "For three months, I'd been working for freelance photographers—living life, earning money, and it all changed with one left-hand turn." That moment marked the end of her driving, reading regular print, and focusing a camera. She would later see it also as the event that marked the beginning of her own photography business.

"My sister was driving me to a shoot one morning," she recalls, "and I suddenly asked her, 'What do you think of the name Miracle Images?'" After all, if the picture's in focus, it will be a miracle!" Miracle Images became the name of her company and its motto, and that spirit of turning a possible limitation to advantage has been a recurring theme in building her business.

Although focusing is difficult, composition and lighting are her strong suits. Her visual impairment is what Parks believes has helped make her a good photographer in the line she has chosen. "I see the overall design of the picture," she explains, "but I don't get overwhelmed by the tiny details because I can't see them."

Her specialties are landscapes and architecture, images in which her two-dimensional vision is an asset rather than a liability. Parks photographs buildings and construction sites that are often used by companies in brochures and slide presentations. Her favorite camera is a large-format camera, referred to in the photography business as a four-by-five, because it has a 4-by-5-inch lens and shoots pictures on individual sheets of film, rather than on a roll. The large lens makes it possible for Parks to see well enough to frame an image before shooting it and thus to get the picture she wants.

After four years, her pool of clients is both impressive and growing. Parks has provided high-quality products and services to GBBM Architects, City of Hamilton Economic Development Department, Hamilton Chamber of Commerce, *Cincinnati* magazine, *Dayton Monthly* magazine, DH Architects, Miles McClellan Construction, and the YMCA. Her customers are pleased with her photographs and pass her name along to others.

Her office is a spare bedroom in her home, where she has a closed-circuit television (CCTV) and other magnifiers, as well as a computer equipped with ZoomText Xtra screen magnification software by Ai Squared. She keeps her own records, producing everything, including invoices, in 18- or 20-point type.

One of the best parts of her job, Parks says, is that she is often working outdoors in the sunlight while others are behind desks indoors. Although her early work in public relations was not her dream job, she is quick to point out that the experience serves her well now that she is in business for herself.

As a member of two professional organizations for builders, construction designers, and engineers, Parks makes it her business to establish contacts, build personal relationships, and solicit business with potential clients. She writes and sends press releases about her story to television stations and newspapers (an effort that has netted considerable press) and promotes her work by exhibiting in art shows.

"You have to call prospective clients whether you like doing it or not," she advises would-be entrepreneurs. "You have to follow up every lead, make every possible contact. I don't expect anybody to call and say 'I have a $200,000 grant for you, do you want it?' It's up to me to make those calls, do the research, go after the business."

In addition to initiative, Parks believes that self-discipline and the ability to solve problems creatively are essential qualifications for establishing a business. If a piece of equipment fails or a driver does not show up, a self-employed person needs to be creative in finding a quick solution.

Parks has all the qualities she recommends: initiative, self-discipline, and creativity. She is her own publicist, marketer, and accountant. Her two dream projects, she says, are to compile enough photographs for a book of the capital buildings in all 50 states and for a book of churches, historic and modern. There is little reason to doubt that she will accomplish whatever she sets out to do.

THREE TIPS FOR SUCCESS
1. Obtain formal training in your chosen profession. As Parks says, "It would have taken a lifetime to learn about photography what I learned in a few short years in school."
2. Join a professional or trade organization. "I wouldn't be in business without the referrals I get from the Society for Marketing Professional Services," Parks notes.
3. Take formal business classes. "You can't run your own business without learning how to market yourself and write a business plan," Parks emphasizes.

ADAPTIVE EQUIPMENT: A computer equipped with ZoomText Xtra magnification software by Ai Squared; a CCTV and handheld magnifiers; a Nikon monocular for reading Walk signs and street signs when traveling independently; and a white cane, used only in crowded, unfamiliar environments. (See the Resources section at the end of this book.)

TOOLS OF THE TRADE: A Nikon N90s 35mm camera with a Nikkor 28–85mm zoom lens; a Hasselblad medium-format camera with two lenses (a Zeiss

120mm lens and a Zeiss 50mm lens); two film backs and a Polaroid back; a Sinar 4 x 5 camera with bag bellows and two lenses (a Sinar 150mm lens and a Sinar 90mm lens) and a Polaroid 4 x 5 film back; a Bogen tripod; a Sekonic light meter; and a Dyna-Lite electronic flash kit, which includes two power packs and three light heads. Lighting equipment also includes two reflectors, a spot-grid kit, two umbrellas, a radio slave, and six light stands.

SALARY: Gross receipts for 1999 were $17,000. Parks estimates that in another three years, she will receive double that amount.

ABOUT NOEL RUNYAN

BUSINESS
Personal Data Systems

LOCATION
Campbell, California

AGE
51

CAUSE OF VISUAL IMPAIRMENT
An accident with explosives

VISUAL ACUITY
Total blindness

BUILDER OF ADAPTIVE COMPUTER SYSTEMS

Noel Runyan

"I'm not always the best businessperson, but I'm doing what I want to do."

NOEL RUNYAN HAS ALWAYS HAD a passion for understanding how things work and inventing new approaches to problems. You might say that passion cost him his eyesight, when as a curious teenager, he decided to surprise his friends and family with a huge Fourth of July boom. You might also say that, as an adult, that passion has earned him a place of legendary stature among blind computer users nationwide.

Runyan was 16 years old when he suddenly and dramatically lost his sight in his hometown of Los Alamos, New Mexico, as the result of experimenting with explosives. The better part of his junior year in high school was spent in the hospital and ended with a two-month crash course at the New Mexico School for the Blind in braille, orientation and mobility, and how to adapt to life as a blind person. It was not long before he was dazzling everyone around him with his ingenuity, inventiveness, and desire to help others.

His first job after he graduated from college in 1973 was with IBM, where he worked on a special task force to develop myriad technologies to help people with disabilities. His ideas grew into prototypes for typewriters that talked, calculators with braille, and some early speech output from computers.

The mission at the time was to develop a tactile CRT (computer screen) equivalent, which led Runyan and his colleagues down many interesting side roads. "We looked at all sorts of ways of tickling people's fingers," he says, "and developed some 87 technologies. What we were looking for back then was a full-page braille display." While some of the prototypes led to later products, and other, singular models were used by particular employees, the net result for Runyan was to be honored for "best contribution" to the company. The award included a trip to Hawaii, and he recalls deciding on the return flight that it was time to find a way to fulfill his dream of truly serving other people who are blind.

For the next five years, Runyan worked with Telesensory Systems in Mountain View, California, which was then on the cutting edge of computer technology for blind people. One of his groundbreaking contributions there was to recognize that the original VersaBraille, the machine that would serve as the first computer for blind people around the world, could be far more than a reading machine. VersaBraille was a tape-based machine with a braille display, and Runyan recognized that with the addition of a serial interface, it could become a word processor as well, a computer device from which people who were blind could print their own notes and documents.

Since 1983, however, Runyan and his wife, Debby, have been in business for themselves, originally selling and ultimately building, customizing, and perfecting computer systems for blind customers.

Personal Data Systems, about a mile from the Runyans' home, is where Runyan can be found each day building systems, shipping products for sale, providing customer support, and developing personal tutorials for individual customers. Although Runyan once had a staff of six, his wife gradually learned and assumed duties in various departments, so that the couple now do everything themselves. The division of labor, Runyan says, is much like the division of labor in a household: Both are capable of doing most things; each generally does what is most efficient. Bookkeeping, for example, was once done by Runyan, but is now more efficiently handled by his wife, who is sighted.

He quips: "I'm the president in charge of the company; she's the vice president in charge of everything else!" In a more serious vein, Runyan believes that the ability to run the company as equal partners, to find a balance and maintain stability, is one of their major accomplishments. "You have to back each other up," he says.

Runyan is a born inventor and risk taker. When he decided to become his own employer, the object was research and development. He built—and marketed—the Audapter, a speech synthesizer that was a milestone in its time; its quicker response time and lower price made it a popular alternative to DECtalk by SMART Modular Technologies. He was so knowledgeable about technology and making programs work with speech that customers who purchased the Audapter began to ask him for other things, too. Some wanted him to build systems, and others wanted his help in finding the best assistive technology products.

Eventually, Runyan found himself in the business of sales as well—recommending and selling hardware and software that he personally found useful. He also wrote simple programs that made existing products easier to use. One such program, EasyScan, provided one-touch scanning for users of the early Arkenstone reading systems, a breakthrough at the time. He licensed the program to Arkenstone, and although more sophisticated programs have since been developed, he still occasionally receives royalties. Another program, BuckScan, was the first to enable a blind person to lay a piece of paper currency on the scanner glass and have the Arkenstone reading system announce its value. Still another program, PicTac, produced simple raised-line drawings from scanned print graphics.

As Runyan talked to customers and sold products, always fine-tuning and tweaking hardware to do this or that for individuals, his customized-systems business took on a life of its own and is now the one for which Runyan is most widely known.

"First, it was tech heads who asked me to build things according to their specifications," he says, but eventually his customers included people with a wide range of skill levels and needs. Today, he may design a simple system just to read print and send E-mail for a retired homemaker, then follow this setup with an intricate one incorporating several complex applications for a fast-paced professional.

Attention to detail is his trademark. Moreover, any system that Runyan sets up is completely integrated. That is, single keystrokes bring up programs exactly as the customer has defined the need for using those programs; all disks and devices are neatly labeled in braille; braille command summaries are supplied for easy reference; and a "tour" of the system in a personalized tutorial format is recorded in Runyan's own voice.

This born inventor and problem solver loves a challenge. He cites his number-one hobby, performing magic tricks, as an example of the joy he finds in accomplishing new goals.

When Runyan lost his sight, he recalls, it was difficult to know what was and was not possible. He did not have any blind role models and comments that sighted people are too often "amazed if you can tie your shoe."

Performing magic tricks had been a pastime before he lost his sight. However, Runyan gave up magic when he became blind because he thought of it as an endeavor reserved for sighted people—until he became friends with a colleague at IBM who was a part-time magician. Then Runyan put magic back into his literal bag of tricks and has been perfecting the art for two decades.

Runyan performs what is called intimate magic or parlor magic—done with a few people or in a living room—rather than stage shows, in which, he explains, visual angles are more difficult to control. At many children's birthday parties and meetings of scout troops, he has been the star magician and has dazzled his own children's classmates with balloon animals and sleights-of-hand. He takes particular pleasure in finding tricks that other blind people can appreciate. Vanishing tricks, telepathy tricks, and his favorite—pulling a knotted rope through a block of wood—can all be appreciated without sight. Magic for friends who are blind is completely hands-on, as he invites them to keep track of every step of a trick by touch.

At conferences, Runyan often carries a few balloons in his pocket. You never know when the person sitting next to you may have a baby who needs amusing, he notes.

"I'm not always the best businessperson," Runyan says, "but I'm doing what I want to do." When new customers call for information or advice or existing ones call for technical assistance, he recognizes that he often gives away blocks of time for which a sterner business owner would charge. Yet, he is satisfied that he is providing a high-quality service and customer satisfaction.

Many of his former customers have gone on to set up small businesses themselves, and others have come back for three or four new systems over the years. For example, in the mid-1980s, a busy young lawyer called Runyan for help. He had spilled coffee in his VersaBraille, and if he could not get the legal documents out of it by five o'clock, his client would go to jail. Runyan suggested putting the unit on a heating pad and turning a hair dryer on it—knowing that the best that could be expected would be a few minutes of usefulness. The customer called back, he reports, to say "You have free legal advice for a year!" and has been a repeat customer many times since.

"There are days when it's not fun," Runyan admits. "Usually, when [people call] for customer support they're already at the point of tearing their hair out. They've been trying everything they can think of for three or four hours. Then they call us and are almost too wound up to describe the problem." Those are the phone calls his wife passes to him, he says, as part of their overall balanced relationship.

THREE TIPS FOR SUCCESS
1. Be tenacious. You have to be able to "hang in" even when you are fed up. Do not allow yourself to make a decision at the end of the day; it is too easy to quit. Rest and then get back to it.
2. Prepare yourself with the skills needed to be able to be independent. Even though there may be things you will not have to do, learn to do every-

thing involved in the business, so you know you can rely on yourself if necessary.
3. The ability to work well with people is essential. Work toward being interdependent, rather than dependent. The best work is done as part of a team.

ADAPTIVE EQUIPMENT: A little bit of everything: speech output—VocalEyes, Window-Eyes by GW Micro, and Henter-Joyce's JAWS screen readers; an Audapter speech synthesizer by Personal Data Systems and a DECtalk speech synthesizer by SMART Modular Technologies; an Arkenstone Open Book optical character recognition system; a Braille Blazer by Blazie Engineering for braille embossing (with American Thermoform Braillon in tractor-fed sheets for labeling systems); Internet Explorer; Microsoft Outlook; and Eudora. Sometimes Navigator braille displays, sometimes Powerbraille. (See the Resources section at the end of this book.)

SALARY: In the range of $50,000 to $60,000 per year.

ABOUT CHARLENE COOK

BUSINESS
Crantford's Flowers

LOCATION
Portland, Oregon

AGE
51

CAUSE OF VISUAL IMPAIRMENT
Retinitis pigmentosa

VISUAL ACUITY
Slight peripheral vision and light perception

FLOWER SHOP OWNER
Charlene Cook

"Business is about business. It's not about blindness. People don't need to know that things take you longer or that certain things are harder because you're blind."

WHEN SHE WAS 17, Charlene Cook was, as she describes herself, "a blind girl with an attitude." Her vision, which had never been good, had gotten worse. She could not drive or read print and was pretty angry at the world. At a summer youth program at the Oregon Commission for the Blind, a counselor who was blind took a special interest in her and imparted a healthy dose of his own "go-after-what-you-want-in-life" perspective. With his encouragement, Cook began to take her braille lessons more seriously, and by the end of the summer could read and write braille competently. She enrolled in training for the Business Enterprise Program—a national program operated in every state that prepares blind and visually impaired individuals to run vending facilities, ranging from candy and soda machines to full-service cafeterias, in federally-owned buildings. She was on her way to becoming a successful businesswoman.

Through the Business Enterprise Program, Cook owned and operated three coffee shops over 15 years. Her shops were simple businesses, which served soups, salads, and coffee, with her own homemade soups center stage. "That program was very good to me," she says, "both financially and because it was a lot of fun."

She learned a great deal about operating a business in the 15 years, and in 1985 she and her husband, Curt Cook, decided to look around for a business of their own, one they could operate together as private business owners instead of as part of the Business Enterprise Program. Charlene's father was selling Crantford's Flowers, a business that offered the couple an excellent opportunity to pool their talents and resources. This was not a sentimental matter of keeping a business in the family; rather, Charlene's father had owned the shop for a while and was ready to sell.

"We bought ourselves a job," Cook quips. "We didn't really know anything about the flower business in the beginning, but the phone kept ringing and orders were coming in!" Her husband had an artistic background and took additional courses in floral design, and Cook knew how to run a business.

Crantford's Flowers was founded in 1921 by Mr. and Mrs. Crantford, who sold the business about 50 years later to Charlene Cook's father, who sold it to the Cooks in 1985. Having only three owners in 80 years is good for business, as is being in a prime location and offering a great product.

Early in the successful new venture, however, Cook felt a certain uneasiness about her lack of direct connection to her business. In her coffee shops, she recalls, she was a one-woman show. "In the food business, everything was mine. I cooked, I cleaned, I prepared the food, I kept the books. Now, I'd come to the flower shop, and everything in the shop was print, and I couldn't read it. All I had was this talking calculator and a Perkins Brailler!"

In response to her search for an accessible computer, people would initially ask why Cook did not just hire people to do everything she needed to have done—payroll and accounting, for example—and just be a manager. The idea of having others run her business while she just "found out at the end of year how I did," was far from her notion of how she wanted to run her business.

Cook went to San Francisco, where she had heard there was a computer training center, and began talking to experts on technology. She bought a Vert Plus speech synthesizer and put it in a computer. She learned about the Imprint (which enables the user to write on a Perkins Brailler and produce a printed translation) and added that to her office, too. She also acquired software called Rosebud—a database program specifically designed for florists that enables her to track every order, customer, and payment history—and before long, she had truly taken charge of her shop. She now manages all accounting, bookkeeping, and inventory. A large part of her 40-hour week, however, is spent processing orders over the phone.

"Everyone in the shop can take orders, of course," she explains, "but customer relations are very important in our business, and I like to handle as much of the one-on-one contact myself as possible." She receives those phone orders in her mezzanine office, overlooking the showroom of flowers and gifts. The shop is located on a corner in a 100-year-old established Portland neighborhood, surrounded by trendy shops, with a Starbucks Coffee and a popular bakery just across the street. The huge windows, she says, are good in that shoppers can see in, but a challenge in that they require frequently changed and eye-catching displays.

The shop's premiere products are fresh flowers, but it also carries cards, vases, ornaments, and gifts. Cook attends two to four trade shows a year, taking one trusted employee "who knows my taste and won't attract my attention to anything that wastes my time."

Customer relations is her forte, she says, but she rarely waits on customers on the shop floor. She is not a flower designer, she is quick to assert, and would not be able to see the colors to match a rose to another blossom. "I don't think I'd be a floral designer if I had 20/20 vision," she notes. Her husband is the designer, and there are other employees who do that aspect of the business well.

In the off-season, the shop has four full-time employees in addition to the Cooks. The flower business peaks from October through May, and during those months, as many as 18 additional employees may be brought on board to keep business moving.

Cook has clear notions about the proper place for blindness in business. She advises entrepreneurs to put their blindness on the back burner. "Business is about business," she says; "it's not about blindness. People don't need to know that things take you longer or that certain things are harder because you're blind. You have to be prepared to do as well or better than anybody else. People don't have time to understand that the order isn't [ready] because of blindness."

In keeping with this philosophy, Cook says, many of the customers with whom she has dealt by telephone for years have no idea that she is blind. When it seems relevant to tell them, she does. For example, one long-time customer insisted on the phone that Cook should be the one to design the flowers for her garden party. "You don't want me," Cook told her. "I'm not a designer. I'll send my husband."

When a customer comes in and wants to be served by Cook personally, she always has her white cane in hand. "I want to be sure that the blindness is up front in that situation," she explains, "so there are no awkward moments of confusion." The important matter is to provide service to the customer. "There's no shame in it," she explains. "I don't hide it.... I could bring [blindness] into every transaction, but why? People are often buying flowers for an occasion—a wedding, a funeral, a special event in the family. Our business is about *them*, not me."

When Cook was 17, she had an attitude. She has one now, too: an energetic attitude that incorporates hard work with optimism and success. It has served her well.

THREE TIPS FOR SUCCESS
1. You have to strive to be the best, or as good as or better than anyone else doing the same business. If you think the leg up is your disability and that people will patronize you for it, throw that idea out the window. It is not going to happen.
2. Whatever the business, it has to be your business. Food service was Cook's business, "in the palm of my hand," as she puts it, but the flower business was not at first. Now it is, and it would not be successful without Cook. "If you don't make it your business, it will become someone else's."
3. Remember that nobody cares as much about the success of the business as you do. Never go to work just for something to do.

ADAPTIVE EQUIPMENT: A computer with a speech synthesizer; Imprint, a Perkins Brailler, and a Braille 'n Speak notetaker. (See the Resources section at the end of this book.)

TOOLS OF THE TRADE: The Rosebud database program for florists.

SALARY: A personal salary of more than $50,000 per year.

ABOUT LARRY CHASE

BUSINESS
Chase Online Marketing Strategies

LOCATION
New York, New York

AGE
46

VISUAL ACUITY
No central vision, good peripheral vision

MARKETING CONSULTANT
Larry Chase

"My mental ability to stay focused on the task at hand has been key to my success."

L ARRY CHASE DECIDED LONG AGO that to succeed, he needed to be willing to take risks and to reinvent himself. After working as a radio producer and then a successful copywriter with New York advertising agencies, he did just that, and the results have been stellar.

In 1993, Chase took what he knew from working in marketing and writing advertisements for the corporate sector and launched Chase Online Marketing Strategies. The Internet was where business was headed, he believed, and he wanted to be on the cutting edge of providing direction to businesses that wanted to use the new marketplace well.

"Mine was one of the first two commercial Web sites in New York," he says, appropriately proud that he had the foresight to create www.chaseonline.com when the concept of company Web sites was still in its infancy. Today, his international business has three major components: an online newsletter, a marketing consultancy, and a speaking itinerary. All three are markedly successful.

Chase is a stern taskmaster, for himself and others, so that 80-hour workweeks are the norm and 18-day work marathons are sometimes necessary. He is relentless, focused, and smart.

His online newsletter, *Web Digest for Marketers,* goes to over 15,000 online businesses and is one of the few online publications that "makes a tidy profit." Advertising revenue, together with the consulting clients and speaking engagements that instantly payoff by putting his name in the E-mail boxes of corporate leaders worldwide, add up to a biweekly publication credited with 70 percent of his company's revenue.

Chase offers—and delivers—a customized marketing service to companies that can be as "intimate as a roundtable of CEOs or as large as a circus tent of 1,000 people." By researching the kind of service a company provides and studying its competition, he offers solid guidelines for maximizing the power of the World Wide Web as a marketing tool. He has made presentations in locales as varied as Sweden, Toronto, California, and Washington, DC, and counts among his clients such Fortune 500 companies as Con Edison, 3Com, New York Life, and Digital Equipment Corporation.

His book, *Essential Business Tactics for the Net,* published by John Wiley & Sons in 1998, became a best-seller in its field in just one year, is in its fourth printing, and has been excerpted in six magazines. Like so many other examples of Chase's success, it has done well largely because he is a master of recognizing opportunities and seizing them.

On his Web site, Chase offers a sample of the book and the opportunity to buy it in quantity. He also offers samples of his newsletter and invites businesses to subscribe to it free of charge. By providing the newsletter at no cost to subscribers, he says he automatically develops "inbound leads." In other words, businesses provide their E-mail address and see his newsletter—promoting Chase Marketing Strategies and its consulting services—and become accustomed to associating the name of his company with expertise in marketing. When they need marketing expertise, his is the first name to come to mind. By syndicating portions of his newsletter to other business publications, he again gets his company's name before the eyes of countless executives who often become clients.

Chase views his visual impairment as both an asset and a liability. Because of his inability to see conventional print, he moved into the world of computers ahead of many of his peers. "I needed video magnification when I worked at the ad agency," he explains. "Secretaries couldn't spell. I was handing in copy I couldn't read." Thus, his visual impairment led him early to video magnifiers and ultimately to a computer screen with software for magnification. When he discovered the Internet, it occurred to him that, using a computer, almost anything he needed to read could be magnified.

41

"On the one hand," he muses, "my vision makes it much more difficult to read what I need and makes me slower; on the other hand, in reaching my long-range goals, my vision served as a catalyst to speed me ahead of the rest of the population."

Chase estimates that reading the voluminous amount of data required for him to stay on top of his field probably takes him three times longer than it would a sighted person. To accomplish the task, he uses a variety of methods. On his computer, he uses ZoomText Xtra, Level Two software that both magnifies the text and provides speech output simultaneously. He pays readers at least $150 a week to read material that is not available online and uses audiotapes from such sources as Recording for the Blind and Dyslexic (RFB&D) and the National Library Service for the Blind and Physically Handicapped. "When my book was published," he recalls, "the very first two books out of my box of authors' copies were for me and my associate. The next two were shipped to RFB&D to be recorded for people who can't read print."

As an expert on online marketing trends, Chase has been quoted in *The New York Times, Business Week, USA Today,* and a host of other business-related publications. His book and his marketing strategies have been featured on CNN, CBS, and elsewhere in electronic media. These results, he says, come directly from the intense self-discipline of always focusing.

"It's ironic," he points out, "that my physical eyesight includes minimal central vision. Yet, my mental ability to stay focused on the task at hand has been key to my success."

Sometimes, the learning curve has meant some tough breaks for Chase's business. In 1994, for example, Chase was featured in a *BusinessWeek* cover story, "How the Internet Will Change Your Business," and the response from potential clients was overwhelming. He was not experienced enough then, he says, to handle the influx of calls and so lost sales.

Today, he knows much better. A number of freelance editors and Web researchers work for him, writing the newsletters and checking out the Internet business of his clients' competitors. He has 600 other Web sites that are linked to his home page and has more business than he can handle.

Today, he turns business away but, as he says, "that's a quality problem to have."

THREE TIPS FOR SUCCESS

1. Find your passion before you set up a business because you will probably go through hell on your way to success, and it may as well be for something you are passionate about doing.
2. Do not be afraid to reinvent yourself. Chase was a radio producer, award-winning copywriter, and executive recruiter before he became the president of his own company. Each career meant rein-

venting himself in professional terms, a skill he says is a necessity in today's marketplace.

3. Maintain an absolute focus. Particularly with a visual impairment, it is too easy, without persistence and perseverance, to allow oneself to get lost on a tangent.

ADAPTIVE EQUIPMENT: A standard Pentium II PC with ZoomText Xtra by Ai Squared for screen magnification and speech output. (See the Resources section at the end of this book.)

SALARY: Chase charges $300 per hour for consulting.

ABOUT CARLA HAYES

BUSINESS
Lengua-Learn Communications

LOCATION
McMurray, Pennsylvania

AGE
40

CAUSE OF VISUAL IMPAIRMENT
A damaged optic nerve from birth; later retinitis
pigmentosa

VISUAL ACUITY
Light perception

FOREIGN LANGUAGE TUTOR AND TRANSLATOR

Carla Hayes

*"If you had told me in college
that I would go into business for myself,
I would have laughed."*

W HEN CARLA HAYES was laid off from her full-time teaching job 10 years ago because of budget cutbacks, she fell back on other skills to generate income. When she landed another teaching position a short time later, she had already tasted the freedom of owning her own business and had no intention of giving it up. She has the best of all worlds, she says, teaching half-time and running her own business as well.

Teaching foreign languages to children has long been her specialty, but Hayes was concerned early in her teaching career that if she taught only children, she would lose her upper-level language skills. She began private tutoring in French, Spanish, and German. Eventually, she began to offer translation services, teaching English as a second language and communications seminars in the corporate sector. Ten years ago, her business, Lengua-Learn Communications, was born, and the range of opportunities it has led to is many and varied indeed.

In any given month, Hayes may tutor as many as ten private students in three different languages, translate legal documents for a physician who is purchasing a condominium in Mexico, or develop study sheets of the most frequently used trade phrases for a particular industry that needs to communicate in German, French, or Spanish.

One repeat customer, for example, is J. C. Penney's collections office, located in Pennsylvania, whose service representatives frequently need to discuss accounts with Spanish-speaking customers. With each newly hired batch of customer service representatives, Hayes prepares to teach another class. Students learn basic conversational Spanish, as well as frequently required phrases of the job, such as "Your bill is overdue"; "You owe x amount of money"; or "If you don't pay, we will have to go to a collection agency."

The increasing number of parents who are choosing to home school their children is another source of more business for Lengua-Learn Communications. Hayes often works with a consortium of home-schooling families, who join forces to hire her as foreign language teacher for a while to help high school students meet state foreign language requirements. That involvement has piqued yet another new interest, evaluating home-school students, a formal process that requires special state certification that Hayes is currently seeking.

Hayes says of herself "I bore easily," and evidence of that truth is clear in her myriad interests and talents. Initially a music major in college, she continues to play the organ and keyboard (often performing for weddings and other special occasions). She switched to a triple major in Spanish, French, and German, with a minor in speech and broadcasting. Over the years, Hayes has built a small recording studio at home—with professional recording equipment, microphones, and mixers. There she has produced newsletters for the Independent Visually Impaired Enterprisers, a group in which she has been involved for 10 years. She is currently in her last term as president.

Teaching others to communicate in a second language naturally blended with her personal focus on communication of all sorts. Thus, the idea was born to begin consulting as a communications expert to corporations and groups. Hayes wrote, narrated, and produced *Dynamic Communications,* an audiocassette presentation, with help from engineers. She composed and produced the music for the product in her home studio and has sold the set to students, executives, and politicians. She now markets her Dynamic Communications presentations to corporations, selling tapes, of course, at the end of her workshops.

"If you had told me in college that I would go into business for myself," Hayes reflects, "I would have laughed. I had no desire to go into business and had no classes [in business]. The only business school I've attended is the school of hard knocks, and I've learned quite a lot in that school."

As a blind business owner, Hayes says planning ahead has always been a key strategy for her. When it looks like translation, tutoring, or other business will be winding up soon, she places an advertisement in the local business publication or starts telephoning former clients. She joined the Chamber of Commerce and exhibits her products and services at educational conventions, home schoolers' conventions, and local trade shows when appropriate and affordable.

"I try to make lemonade out of lemons," she says, explaining her response to hard times, "and I keep moving because I have a mean boss!" When business is slow, she develops new products, such as an employment test, the EQ (Employability Quotient), which she has used in workshops and is now packaging for sale. The EQ has 78 questions for rating one's strengths and weaknesses and comes with a complete scoring analysis.

Hayes believes that her training as a teacher has been invaluable in running her own business, since she learned how to prepare overhead transparencies, handouts, and presentation notes. Today, in both her teaching and business endeavors, she works exclusively from braille notes after she composes all presentation materials on her speech-equipped computer. When customers give her foreign language materials for translation, she asks for documents on disk and reads them with her computer, or if the documents are in print, she reads them with her optical character recognition software, which is capable of reading foreign languages.

Hayes keeps all financial records initially in braille and then has readers transfer accounting information to print ledgers. She prepares invoices and accounting summaries on her computer. "The more I do myself," she explains, "the less money I have to give the accountant."

Since that layoff 10 years ago, she has been offered full-time teaching positions. Turning them down was not a hard decision to make—her half-time job, she notes, keeps up her teaching skills and gives her the freedom to pursue an endless stream of fascinating business pursuits.

"One thing about blindness," she says, "is that we are conditioned to believe that we are inferior. We need to look at the positive side of that facet of our personalities. We are not distracted by sight and have many advantages. You have to hit the valleys to appreciate the mountains." Hayes has done so, and her perseverance is a sparkling example of the value of self-confidence.

THREE TIPS FOR SUCCESS

1. When you are setting up any business, start part time to make sure you really like it and can do it before you invest a lot of capital and throw caution to the wind.

2. You need to discover what it is that you *like* to do and do well, not just go after the money. If you are not having fun, you will not get much done.
3. Perseverance is the name of the game. You just have to keep at it, even on days when you do not feel like doing so. Do not let anybody tell you that you cannot do it.

ADAPTIVE EQUIPMENT: A Pentium computer with dual-boot DOS and Windows setup, with Henter-Joyce's JAWS for DOS and Alva Access Group's out-Spoken for Windows access software; a 40-cell Alva ABT40 refreshable-braille display for reading computer output on her desktop system; JAWS for speech output on the laptop she carries on-site; a Blazie Braille Lite notetaker for keeping daily notes and phone numbers; and TeleSensory Corporation's Reading AdvantEdge software for reading printed documents. (See the Resources section at the end of this book.)

TOOLS OF THE TRADE: A four-track Marantz professional recorder and a Yamaha keyboard for composing and producing music in her recording studio, and foreign-language dictionaries on CD-ROM disks that include lexicons to which words can be added.

SALARY: Fees vary widely, depending on the nature of the work. For tutoring, she has charged $15 to $30 per hour, and for corporate workshops, $150 per hour.

ABOUT STEVE HANAMURA

BUSINESS
Hanamura Consulting

LOCATION
Beaverton, Oregon

AGE
55

VISUAL IMPAIRMENT
Congenitally blind

VISUAL ACUITY
Light perception

DIVERSITY AND LEADERSHIP TRAINING CONSULTANT

Steve Hanamura

"I used to want to prove that I could be somebody, to be the best. That attitude won't get you very far. Now, I just want to do my best."

CONCOURSE B AND C of Chicago's O'Hare Airport are Steve Hanamura's playground. Hanamura does not live in Chicago, he lives in Oregon, but in his fast-paced consulting and training business, where "time is money" and flight is efficiency, O'Hare is an environment he has come to know well. In a given week, Hanamura may travel to three cities in three days; go back to the home office in Beaverton, Oregon, to make proposals to clients for seminars in three to four months; or do a half-day training program across town. He is a serene, spiritual man with a smorgasbord of messages for the corporate world, and the blend has spelled success since 1987.

Hanamura's business is a one-man show—offering diversity training, leadership development, and team building to companies and organizations nationwide. Unlike some individual consultants, Hanamura did not start out by doing something he liked and gradually watch it grow into a business; rather, he saw early in his career that to have the life he wanted to have, he would have to strive for self-employment, to become a consultant—a job that would enable him to travel and to set his own schedule.

His job fresh out of school (he has a bachelor's degree in psychology from Linfield College in McMinnville, Oregon, and a master's degree in counseling from the University of Oregon) was as a college counselor. "Growing up, I always missed my family," he says. We lived east of Los Angeles, and because I was blind, I went away to school in Berkeley, California. I saw my family twice a year. With a 10-month college counseling contract, I saw them even less."

After Hanamura married and had children of his own, time became even more precious to him. He realized that when he had to travel for work, he sometimes went near his parents' home and could arrange a bonus visit. Thus, he realized early that becoming a consultant would give him the freedom he wanted to put his family first.

Hanamura had a vision of where he wanted to go and began to work strategically toward his goal. He wanted to be a consultant who would travel, provide training, and command high fees. He concluded that with the right kind of experience, it would take him about 10 years to position himself to realize that vision. His time would then be more flexible, and

56

he would be in control of it. He knew that he would need credibility in both the corporate and governmental sectors to build a consultancy business, so he investigated jobs in those areas. His career path took him from college counseling to employee relations in banking entities to directing the Client Assistance Program in Oregon and the orientation center of the Oregon Commission for the Blind.

"I now had experience and credibility with institutions of higher learning, corporate, and government agencies," he says, and was thus ready to launch himself as a consultant. Hanamura joined the American Society for Training and Development (ASTD), a national organization of trainers and consultants. Through the organization, he learned how to run a consulting business and met people who were already successful in the area he wanted to pursue: speaking, consulting, and presenting to corporations. When he became president of the local ASTD chapter in 1987, part of the privilege was to conduct a workshop at the organization's national conference. That year, the national ASTD conference was held in Atlanta, Georgia, and Hanamura gave his first presentation there on working with people who are different. The presentation immediately landed him his first three contracts for the same workshop—with the U.S. Navy, the U.S. Army, and the city of Winston-Salem, North Carolina.

In 1988, ASTD presented him with the Multicultural Trainer of the Year award, which further helped him position himself for his strategic vision. That year, Hanamura was hired by Digital Equipment Corporation, Levi Strauss, and U.S. West (which has telephone companies in 14 states). Business continued to mushroom from there, and within three years he was making a six-figure salary. With his success has come a candid appraisal of his own image and the impression he makes on others. In this society, he says, "the darker you are, the greater the discrimination." Yet, in his case, he believes that his Asian American status is canceled by his blindness. In other words, "there are no boardrooms I couldn't enter now because I'm Asian, but there are boardrooms where I won't get in because I'm blind."

Still, Hanamura believes that blindness is part of the package that you have to integrate into the rest of your being and see it for the mixed blessing that it can be. "There was a time when I was mad at God," he reflects, "because my blindness meant I had to go away to school and couldn't be with my parents." On the other hand, "because of my blindness and success and knowing Gil Johnson at the American Foundation for the Blind, I was able to meet the manager of the San Francisco Giants!"

Hanamura has also developed a careful strategy for putting blindness in its proper perspective when on the road. Although he sometimes takes an employee or family member along, he usually travels to jobs alone, which means that he has to navigate unfamiliar environments independently.

"When I get to a new hotel," Hanamura explains, "I pay the bellhop to give me a quick O&M [orientation and mobility] lesson. I build relationships with service staff and use room service often. . . . Companies aren't paying me to worry about my personal blindness issues. I have to get the blindness stuff out of the way, so that I'm ready to give 100 percent to the business reason that I'm there."

In conducting the business part—that is, workshops and training sessions—Hanamura uses a variety of overhead transparencies, handouts, and videos. He asks for an assistant to operate the visual accompaniments to his presentation, since, again, he believes that getting bogged down in difficulties related to blindness would diminish his overall impact.

Although he enjoys his work, Hanamura does not live for it. "You've got to have balance in your life," he says. "Mine revolves around church, family, and running. The job is the vehicle that helps me do these things."

Hanamura's attitude toward running a marathon reflects his changed attitude toward business. "I used to want to prove that I could be somebody," he says, "to be the best. That attitude won't get you very far. Now, I just want to *do* my best and realize that the glory of everything I do really goes to God."

Whether the subject at hand is diversity, leadership, or life in the 21st century, Hanamura has a network of chief executive officers in nearly every field around the country who recommend him to one another, which accounts for much of his business. "To be successful," he says, "you have to surround yourself with successful people." He has done just that—and so have the lucky people who are around *him*.

THREE TIPS FOR SUCCESS
1. God, family, and friends have always been Hanamura's highest priorities and greatest support.
2. You need to have a vision of where you want to go, the discipline to work toward it, and the ability to delay gratification.
3. Allow others to help you. The Oregon Commission for the Blind, in Hanamura's case, was one tremendous source of help.

ADAPTIVE EQUIPMENT: A Braille 'n Speak note-taker with a disk drive by Blazie Engineering, a computer with Henter-Joyce's JAWS for Windows screen reader, and Duxbury System's Duxbury braille translator. "My main tools are still a Perkins Brailler, a typewriter, a white cane, my mouth, my heart, and my brain," says Hanamura. "I'm determined to become more computer literate as we begin a new century!" (See the Resources section at the end of this book.)

SALARY: Generally, $40,000–$60,000 per year, but fluctuates with the number of clients from nothing to up to six figures.

ABOUT ANN MORRIS

BUSINESS
Ann Morris Enterprises

LOCATION
East Meadow, New York

AGE
48

CAUSE OF VISUAL IMPAIRMENT
Retrolental fibroplasia

VISUAL ACUITY
Total blindness

OWNER OF A MAIL-ORDER BUSINESS SPECIALIZING IN MAINSTREAM AND ADAPTIVE PRODUCTS FOR PEOPLE WITH DISABILITIES

Ann Morris

"My work is my life."

WHEN ANN MORRIS LOST what little sight she had, she had just completed her first year of college. She had struggled throughout her school career with large-print books and audiotapes, but at age 19, she was totally blind. She returned to school, but panicked and dropped out to work in a factory.

Morris's attitude toward blindness is dramatically better 30 years later, and so is her employment status. After she taught herself braille with the help of a correspondence course from the Hadley School for the Blind, raised children, and did a variety of both paid and volunteer jobs, she began her own business almost by accident.

Morris had an idea that perhaps she should market a device she had developed for her own use to other blind people. Called the Optaguide, her 1986 debut product was an accessory to the Optacon, a machine that converted printed characters into tactile form. With the Optaguide, the blind user could independently place Xs and checkmarks in the right spaces on a page while filling out forms. Morris conceived the idea and found others to help her execute it. She advertised in publications for people who are blind, selling the product out of her home. Although she had only marginal success with that product, it whetted her appetite for the world of mail order, and she was ready to try something else.

Her next product was an audible battery tester. With a sighted friend's help, Morris adapted an existing product by adding a buzzer and took her first business risk. She ordered 500 battery testers and 500 buzzers and advertised them in the same publications. A rapidly vanishing inventory indicated that her instincts had been right. Identifying products that were useful to her as a blind person and marketing them to other blind people, she concluded, was what she wanted to do. From a friend, she learned of and joined an organization called the Long Island Networking Entrepreneurs, and now credits that step as one of her wisest business moves. There, she learned about the various ways of setting up a business, hired a lawyer, and incorporated the business as Ann Morris Enterprises.

Her first catalog carried 60 items, and her first year in the mail-order business brought in $6,000. Although some might have found that amount discouraging, Morris knew that she was on the right track. Her persistence paid off; today, her company is a household name to most consumers who are blind or visually impaired and is often the first place they check when seeking a solution to a practical problem. In 1999, she did $500,000 in sales, and her catalog carries 850 products.

Any conceivable item that may enable a blind person to function more efficiently or independently at home or at work can be found in the Ann Morris Enterprises catalog. Initially, her focus was on tools for writing and recording—braille writing devices, signature guides, magnifiers of all shapes and sizes, bold-line pens, modified tape recorders for playing Talking Books, and storage products for organizing audiotapes and papers. Myriad gadgets that are sold in gourmet catalogs and novelty shops also provide particular benefits to customers without sight, however, and Morris has made it her business to ferret out those items and make them available to her customers.

"Talking watches and clocks were originally manufactured as novelty items for sighted people," Morris cites as example, but thousands of them have been purchased by people who are blind or visually impaired. Other items in her catalog that were not originally intended for blind consumers include a talking VCR, talking microwave oven, cooking pots and utensils with added convenience and safety features, and organizers for everywhere from filing cabinets to spice racks. Recognizing that transportation and shopping are more difficult for her customers than for sighted consumers, Morris recently added to her catalog gift items and gourmet foods. Although her three employees are sighted, Morris makes sure that every aspect of her business is manageable by a blind person. "All of us work at whatever desk we need to," she explains, referring to the six desks and five work stations where the customer database, inventory, invoicing, and other aspects are primary focal points. Every computer is equipped with a speech synthesizer and screen-access program, so that anyone in the office can do whatever job is necessary.

When an order comes in by telephone, Morris initially writes it up in braille; she then enters it into the computer to produce a print order and invoice. After the order is filled and packaged, it is always checked against the mailing list to be sure the customer has been entered into the customer database to receive an annual catalog. Finally, the package is labeled and added to the pile for the daily United Parcel Service pickup.

Inventory shelves are labeled in print and braille, when necessary, although most of the time Morris has memorized the location of the merchandise. Although she is able to do every aspect of the business herself, her focus is on taking orders, processing invoices, and scouting for new products.

Her husband—who has his own business as an automation engineer—has been involved in Ann Morris Enterprises from the design and manufacturing standpoint. He helped design her first product and several others along the way. Otherwise, he is involved in her business only to the extent that "we are always looking for products. When we go on vacation, go to the store, go out to run an errand—we are always looking for things that could be added to the catalog."

In addition to the casual ongoing search, Morris attends a number of specialty trade shows. Because she has defined her market as a specific segment of the population, Morris says that many marketing techniques that are used by other mail-order houses simply do not apply. Renting mailing lists, for example, is a commonly used strategy for other mail-order businesses. When the target audience is people who are blind or visually impaired, however, there are no lists to rent. Others who have mailing lists typically guard the privacy of their constituents, and mailing lists for more generalized audiences—such as those of large-print book publishers—yield limited responses. What does work, Morris says, is knowing her own market and how to reach it. She advertises regularly in publications for people who are blind or visually impaired and rents exhibit space at numerous conferences that attract blind and visually impaired people. Today, she has a "clean" database of 33,000 customers that has been carefully combed to ensure only one entry per person.

While her three employees have specific duties (bookkeeping, shipping, and so on), Morris says that every person in the office can and does do every job at one point or another. She has a few people who go to trade shows with her to search for new products and others who are paid to search through catalogs. Although she has no blind employees, she subcontracts a fair amount of work to blind people—the production of her catalog on audiocassette, for instance—and distributes a number of products that are designed or manufactured by blind individuals. Among these products are computer games, computer tutorials, and some specialty items that have been made to carry specific pieces of equipment.

Bestsellers at Ann Morris Enterprises are leather accessories—products gathered from a myriad of sources—including everything from leather wallets and purses to backpacks, tote bags, and other organizers.

Although her Web site is moving into the land of E-commerce with the ability to take orders online, Morris believes that telephone orders will continue to be the majority of her sales. Customers enjoy the personal contact with someone who has actually used the product that is being recommended as useful to blind people. The work has been hard since the sale of that first product, but Morris clearly knew where she was headed and has arrived.

THREE TIPS FOR SUCCESS
1. Know your product line.
2. Have a good marketing strategy.
3. Be a workaholic. Morris says of her own addiction to work: "My work is my life. My husband's work is his life. It's something we're hoping to change, but to build business up, sometimes that *is* your life."

ADAPTIVE EQUIPMENT: Five computers, 386s to Pentium IIs, each equipped with either Henter-Joyce's JAWS for Windows screen readers or MicroTalk Software's ASAP for DOS; a program written for her called Store, which generates purchase orders and invoices and tracks inventory; a talking credit-card machine from Discover Company; three Perkins Braillers for taking telephone orders, and a Braille 'n Speak note taker by Blazie Engineering for keeping track of telephone numbers and other data. (See the Resources section at the end of this book.)

SALARY: The volume of sales for 1999 was $500,000.

ABOUT NICK MEDINA

BUSINESS
Medina Tax and Bookkeeping Service

LOCATION
Concord, California

AGE
65

CAUSE OF VISUAL IMPAIRMENT
Incomplete eyes at birth because of his mother's
rubella

VISUAL ACUITY
20/400 (6/120, its metric equivalent) in one eye
only

OWNER OF A TAX-PREPARATION AND BOOKKEEPING SERVICE

Nick Medina

"I like anything that's a challenge."

NICK MEDINA GOT A LATE START going to school, but he has more than made up for that little bit of lost time. He was 11 years old when his parents were informed that there was indeed a school for their blind child, and they prepared to send him there.

Medina had never been away from home. Sheltered in his small Spanish-speaking farm community in the San Luis Valley of southern Colorado, he had not yet learned to speak English. On September 9, 1945, his parents said a teary farewell to him at the Colorado School for the Deaf and Blind, and his courage and eagerness to try new things have flourished ever since.

Eventually, Medina earned a doctorate in administration and special education from Northern Colorado University in Greeley and had a 30-year career teaching at every level from elementary school to college. In the early 1970s he moved to California, and in 1989 retired early from his job with the Walnut Creek school district.

Throughout his teaching career, however, Medina always had a hand in business. His first job after he graduated from high school was selling insurance for Mutual of New York's south Denver office, and there were many other jobs along the way in the world of finance. Early in his teaching career, he supplemented his income by working as a loan officer for a mortgage company, and in 1972, he obtained a real estate license that he only recently allowed to expire. He bought and sold real estate more as an investment pursuit than as a career in selling property, he says, and was satisfied with his success.

Medina knew when he retired from teaching that he would eventually supplement the 45 percent of salary he received as a pension. He did not realize, however, how quickly he would become bored and need to work. Soon after he retired, he asked his wife to read the classified section from the Sunday newspaper. "The only job there that I was qualified to do was with the IRS [Internal Revenue Service]," he recalls, so he telephoned the IRS the next morning and went to work. Initially, his job with the IRS was to work as a telephone representative, but it was not long before he was promoted. "I didn't like that very much," he confesses. "There were certain procedures you had to follow when someone called in for information—you had to work through about 20 questions with them before you could just tell them what they wanted to know."

His next job with the IRS was in Automated Tax Collections (ACS), which Medina found lively with human interaction and outrageous stories. His role was to call individuals and businesses who were behind in paying their taxes and work out payment schedules to satisfy the government. "When people are behind $100,000 or $200,000," he laughs, "they come up with some pretty wild solutions." It was hard to be bored when he was offered a Burger King franchise or a weekend in Hollywood as tax payers attempted to reconcile their debts! Still, what he had hoped and expected to do when becoming an IRS employee was to work as a tax auditor. By 1992, when he saw no prospect of becoming a tax auditor, he decided to go into business for himself.

Medina Tax and Bookkeeping Service was formed in September 1992 and now has over 300 clients. Although Medina is able to read print "by sticking my nose on the page," with the small amount of vision available in one eye, he does all his tax-preparation work with a speech-equipped computer. Going to clients' offices and homes, he carries his Braille Lite notetaker, writing down all pertinent information as the clients give it to him. Back in the office, he pays readers to pore over the tiny print of merchants' receipts or clients' handwritten ledgers and then to provide him with the totals. "Scanners and reading software can do a pretty good job," he explains, "but you can't trust them with numbers."

Braille has always been a supplementary form of communication for him. Medina cannot read braille rapidly, but he has always used it for reviewing notes while speaking in public or presenting reports, and he depends heavily on his Braille Lite for storing clients' tax information and other data. With special eyeglasses made for him 20 years ago, he reads print when necessary. "I guard those glasses with my life," he chuckles, explaining that no one today can make the right prescription for him. The eyeglasses are bifocals—28 power on the bottom, 20 power on top—and, for whatever reason, he says that no one has ever gotten the numbers just right for him again.

With Window-Eyes software and a DECtalk speech synthesizer, however, Medina does most of his work. With Lacerte, a commercially available software package for preparing taxes, he prepares quarterly and annual taxes for individuals, corporations, and partnerships. Representatives of Lacerte, he says, have been wonderful in working with him to configure their software to work properly with his screen access for speech. "When they start telling me to click twice here or there," he laughs, "I just remind them that this is the blind guy calling, and they're pretty good at helping me figure out the extra steps needed to get it done with speech."

Bookkeeping is a smaller part of his business that he hopes to see grow in the coming years. "Clients don't want to let all that information out of their own offices," he explains, "and I can't do spreadsheets on a Braille Lite." He is in the process of equipping a notebook computer with speech to make it possible for him to work on spreadsheets at any location.

To find clients, Medina initially placed an advertisement in the Yellow Pages. During the first few years, that advertisement accounted for 90 percent of his business. Eventually, however, word-of-mouth was a much more effective advertisement. "One air traffic controller came to me to do his taxes," he cites as an example, "and before long, I had nine more from the same office." Another time, a man from the Philippines came to Medina's office because "he thought from my name that I was Filipino." (Actually, Medina explains, his entire community of origin in the San Luis Valley descend from the Spanish exploration party of Francisco Coronado, who settled the area in 1541.) In any case, the customer was satisfied and spread the word to his friends, so that today Medina has a large group of customers who came to California from the Philippines.

Medina has no employees. He pays readers to total receipts on an as-needed basis and often uses his youngest daughter, a certified accountant, whom he also pays to transmit electronic tax filings for him. It is ironic that he has few clients who are either Hispanic or blind. His rationale: "I don't speak much Spanish any more, although I'm not really sure why I have no Hispanic clients. I think I only have four blind clients because so many blind people don't work."

Although the odds of employment are definitely not favorable for blind people as a whole, Medina has created several successful niches for himself in the economic market. While increasing his tax and bookkeeping business, he is always in tune with other possibilities. "I'll keep doing this until something more interesting comes along, probably another 10 to 15 years," he chuckles. "Right now, I'm thinking about ways to use the Internet to make some fast, big bucks. I like anything that's a challenge."

THREE TIPS FOR SUCCESS
1. You have to have a desire to do something and believe in yourself enough to do it.
2. Before you set up a business, make yourself as knowledgeable as you can about your field.
3. You have to have determination: Push, push, push. Set goals and work to achieve them. If one business does not succeed, try something else.

ADAPTIVE EQUIPMENT: A Pentium computer with Windows '95; GW Micro's Window-Eyes screen-access software; a DECtalk speech synthesizer by SMART Modular Technologies; and a Braille Lite notetaker by Blazie Engineering. (See the Resources at the end of this book.)

TOOLS OF THE TRADE: Lacerte tax-preparation software, QuickBooks Pro software for bookkeeping, and a good memory for math.

SALARY: "I'm satisfied," Medina says. Although he would not disclose his salary, he says that someone in a tax and bookkeeping business could reasonably expect to earn $80,000 to $150,000 with hard work and a full-time effort.

ABOUT LOU FIORITTO

BUSINESS
Braille Works International

LOCATION
Tampa, Florida

AGE
52

CAUSE OF VISUAL IMPAIRMENT
Retrolental fibroplasia

VISUAL ACUITY
Total blindness

PRODUCER OF BRAILLE MATERIALS
Lou Fioritto

*"To make the world
a more readable place."*

LOU FIORITTO WAS HAVING DINNER with his wife, Joyce, in a Cleveland restaurant in 1993 when he was handed his first braille menu. "I'd never seen one before and was very interested in how it was done," he recalls. As appreciative as he was as a long-time braille reader to be receiving a menu in braille, his immediate conclusion was that he would have made it differently. "I would have given it a table of contents," he told his wife, as he hunted through the difficult format to find items of interest. "And I would have put it on smaller paper, 8½ by 11 inches, with a plastic comb binding, to make it easier to handle."

Throughout the meal, they continued to talk about the braille menu. "Why don't we do it?" Joyce suggested. As it happened, the employment picture was one enormous question mark for Fioritto at that time. After 11 years with Internal Revenue Service and 10 years in sales and management with MCI and then a business forms company, which went bankrupt, he was out of a job.

"I was blind and 43 and out of work," he sums it up, and employers wanted to hire him for entry-level jobs. Fioritto had held a few unsatisfactory positions, but now, here he was—with a brand-new business idea.

He had never produced braille documents nor set up a business, but the more he talked about the prospect, the more certain he was that producing braille materials as a business venture was a sound idea. He went to the Service Corps of Retired Executives for advice and was assigned two retired executives whom he credits with much of his success today. The executives taught him how to set up a business; made him do research; and, most important, forced him to write a business plan.

Fioritto researched the competition, the market, and the equipment for producing his product. He wrote his business plan, received some assistance with equipment from the Ohio Rehabilitation Services Commission, borrowed money for other equipment, and started hunting for business. He made calls; sent letters; and, in general, approached the sale of braille materials as he would have with any other product.

On the 24th floor of Erieview Office Tower in Cleveland, Ohio, in December 1993, he signed his first contract. The customer was Ameritech, and five documents were to be delivered on January 25, 1994. As the elevator doors closed, he recalls hugging his wife with glee and then realizing: He did not have a braille printer or braille-translation software, and here he was with a deadline a few weeks away.

The Fiorittos bought Megadots braille-translation software and started learning what they needed to know. When the Juliet braille embosser was delivered on January 24, they set to work and delivered the documents on time.

In 1994, Braille Works International billed $7,000 or $8,000. In 1998, gross sales were nearly $200,000 and in 1999, they were about $245,000. Much of the work has been uphill, but Fioritto says he has loved every minute of it.

There were times in the early days, he says now, when he thought the business was going to fold. The Fiorittos had taken a second mortgage to pay for equipment and inventory, and sales were barely paying for paper. Joyce was still working 60 hours a week at her job, and Lou was beginning to accept that it was time to go job hunting again.

While praying for solutions at two o'clock one morning, Fioritto recalls, he decided to look at his old business plan, and the word *restaurants* jumped out at him. He had been pursuing governmental and corporate contracts and had forgotten about his initial target market. The next morning, he woke up his wife and said, "We're going to make it." He spent the day calling restaurant chains.

Today, Fioritto produces braille materials for about 150 regular customers, including corporations, governmental entities, agencies, and restaurants. The majority of his customers, however, are restaurants. Many national restaurant chains among his clientele, such as Cracker Barrel, Applebees, TGI Fridays, and Bob Evans, change menus often and may require as many as 1,200 copies per order.

In 1996, the Fiorittos, along with their business, moved from Cleveland to Tampa, Florida, where, Fioritto says, business has been kind to them. The 800-square-foot office is adjacent to the house but quickly became crowded, so the two-car garage is also used as office space, as are parts of the house. In addition to the Fiorittos, who are both "more than full time," there are two regular employees, two on an as-needed basis, and three high school students who bind braille materials. Braille Works International produces braille, large-print, and recorded materials, subcontracting the narration of recorded materials to two former radio broadcasters who keep the company's professional recorders in their homes.

Whereas he once ordered braille paper and plastic binding combs as needed, Fioritto says he now orders 30,000 combs at a time and purchases 150 cartons of braille paper a year. Bursting pages and removing the tractor-feed sprockets, once done by hand, are now done entirely by machines.

The slogan of the company is "To make the world a more readable place," and Fioritto is always thinking of ways to make it true. Restaurant menus now typically contain large print and braille in one convenient volume, with an acetate cover and contents page, so restaurant patrons can quickly locate desired items. For recorded materials, Fioritto provides a table of contents on cassette, to make the location of specified portions of reading more efficient. "We have so much volume in our lives," he says, "the less we have to carry around and the easier we can make materials to handle, the better."

Joyce's experience as an executive secretary and her design sense have been invaluable in ensuring the visual appeal of products, whereas Lou's experience in sales and as a braille reader has opened countless doors and created satisfied customers. The company has grown to include four braille printers, three computer systems, two GBC binding machines, and laser printers for producing large-print materials. Customers know that they will receive a high-quality product on time and that Lou will work nights and weekends, if necessary, to get the work out. Lou's goal has become a reality, and business is booming. The best part is that as he succeeds, he is making the world a more readable place.

THREE TIPS FOR SUCCESS
1. Believe in a higher power. As Fioritto said, "I don't know how I could do business without my relationship with Christ."
2. Always keep your customers in mind when working on your product.
3. Maintain a strong business sense. If you establish deadlines, keep them. "Sometimes we have to beg for more time," Fioritto notes, "but we can work till 3 A.M. if we have to."

ADAPTIVE EQUIPMENT: Megadots braille-translation software by Duxbury Systems; four braille printers from Enabling Technologies: an Express 100, a Bookmaker, a Juliet, and an Index; two laser printers; a Minolta copier; two GBC binding machines; a bursting machine to separate and strip side sprockets from pages; three Pentium II computer systems, one of which is equipped with Henter-Joyce's JAWS for Windows screen reader; and a Braille Lite 2000 notetaker by Blazie Engineering for all personal notes, orders, and phone numbers. (See the Resources section at the end of this book.)

TOOLS OF THE TRADE: three professional Marantz recorders with microphones and a tape-duplicating machine.

SALARY: Gross receipts were $196,000 in 1999; the Fiorittos probably take about $60,000 a year in salaries.

ABOUT CARLA MCQUILLAN

BUSINESS
Main Street Montessori Association

LOCATION
Springfield, Oregon

AGE
37

CAUSE OF VISUAL IMPAIRMENT
Stargardt's disease, diagnosed at age 10

VISUAL ACUITY
Good peripheral vision; can read large print at a
very close range

DIRECTOR OF A MONTESSORI SCHOOL
Carla McQuillan

"I never hesitated to volunteer to work, to take another's shift, to stay late, to come in early."

WHEN CARLA MCQUILLAN was young, she began wondering what sorts of things she could do as a blind person when she grew up. Her brother was a whiz at electronics; that was out. Her sister was a nurse, so she could not do that either.

She loved children, and books for young children were in large print, easy for her to see. Thus, her initial career path was charted. McQuillan landed a job playing guitar and teaching songs to children in a Montessori school, near California State University in Fullerton where she attended classes. At the Montessori school, she noticed that the children were different from any other children she had known. They were more responsible, well mannered, and creative; took direction better; and were simply "a whole other crop of kids from any I'd known." She decided that "whatever it was that made them behave that way, it was something I wanted to learn."

When she enrolled in the Montessori teacher training program at California State, she could no longer read children's books in large print, so she took courses in storytelling—weaving tales with words and encouraging children to use their imaginations to make pictures in their own minds. Montessori teaching is a perfect match for a teacher who is blind, McQuillan points out. "You never talk to a child from across the room, but get up close— where a blind teacher can easily tell what he or she is doing. All the materials are hands-on, with little strictly visual emphasis."

After teaching in various Montessori schools, McQuillan enrolled at the University of Illinois, where she earned a bachelor's degree in speech communications in 1988, combining performance and interpretation of literature with storytelling and speech communication. The only time she has not been involved with education, she says, was the first 15 months after her daughter, now 16 years old, was born. "I can't sit still for a moment," she says, and believes that she was a better role model for her daughter working even as a teaching assistant and making just enough to pay for child care than she was as a stay-at-home mom.

When the family moved to Oregon in 1990, their second child was only a baby. McQuillan wanted to be with her children, but needed to earn an income as well. The solution was to establish a small Montessori school at home, so the McQuillans bought a house with a separate bedroom, bathroom, and outdoor exit and adequate space for a school. It was not long, however, before McQuillan knew that she wanted a larger school on a separate piece of property.

With a business loan from the National Federation of the Blind, McQuillan leased a building in 1993 and set up a school. For three years, Children's Choice Montessori flourished, and, as McQuillan puts it, "I never bounced a check." In 1996, the Main Street Montessori Association (the umbrella corporation for the school) purchased an acre and constructed its own building for Children's Choice Montessori. Today, there are 120 students in all, ranging in age from 2½ to 8, and as the executive director, McQuillan does just about everything but direct teaching.

A good lawyer and accountant are essential for establishing the best business model for the individual situation, McQuillan believes, and she thinks she had excellent advice on both counts. She and her husband were advised to set up a nonprofit organization as a limited liability company. Although this arrangement means that her salary is not enormous today, it will provide additional income in another 13 years and into her retirement. But retirement is far from the mind of this animated businesswoman.

No two days are alike on the job, McQuillan says, which is what makes it best suited to her energy and creativity. Some days, she deals with the nuts and bolts of collecting tuition, paying bills, and balancing the books, and other days, she works on the school newsletter, arranges field trips, or prepares a hot lunch for 50 children. The kitchen is in her office, and when the cook is absent, McQuillan enjoys preparing the school's typical lunch fare of lasagna, quiche, macaroni and cheese, or quesadillas. "Many of our students might not get a hot meal every day at home," she explains, "so it's important that they get it with us."

Although the tuition is a steep $340 a month, the student population is economically and racially diverse. Some children are in foster homes and receive state aid for tuition, whereas others are from upper-middle-class families. The school also welcomes children with all levels of ability and currently includes two children who are blind, a child with Down syndrome, and a few with developmental disabilities.

A trip to the director's office for a child with unacceptable behavior is not typical either. Parents who remember being sent to the principal's office for punishment may be surprised to find McQuillan holding a "disciplinary problem" on her lap and singing an Irish ballad. "If a child is really out of control," she says, "I restrain him or her on my lap, with a technique ensuring that [the child] won't hurt [himself or herself] or me, and just start singing." The effect is magical. The child becomes calm, reasonable discussions follow, and education goes on.

McQuillan also handles problems her parents or teachers are having. In addition, she gives tours of the school to interested parents and requires all parents to attend regularly scheduled educational sessions that she organizes and conducts.

In 1998, the director of another Montessori school in nearby Cottage Grove, Oregon, retired, and Main Street Montessori Association acquired the school. This school has only 25 students and 3 teachers, and is running smoothly with McQuillan's assistant director serving as head teacher.

There is a great deal of writing to do in running the two schools—newsletters, funding proposals, and correspondence with parents and others. Although she uses a computer with Microsoft Word and ZoomText Xtra for screen enlargement and speech output, McQuillan finds that, for her, the most efficient method of composition is to dictate text to her office manager, who reads it back to her, and then to do some editing.

An atypical aspect of McQuillan's business is that she has incorporated her volunteer work into her work at the school. As president of the National Federation of the Blind (NFB) of Oregon, she found that trying to do at work from home while working all day was not efficient. Now, a part-time assistant in the school is paid specifically to do NFB work, and McQuillan incorporates her work for the NFB with running the school. "All my staff is wonderfully supportive," she asserts.

Blindness is an integral part of life at Children's Choice Montessori. The cook, who is blind, is easily the most popular staff member among the students, McQuillan declares. McQuillan also says that in the summer, "when I run the NFB camp at national [NFB] conventions, some of my staff come along and volunteer their time as counselors and child care providers. It's a culture: I do the school, and I do NFB; it all goes together. My staff have learned a lot about blindness, and that benefits the atmosphere of education for the children."

Her son is a student at the school, although his mother has not been his teacher. As much as she loved teaching, McQuillan says, it is more efficient to find a substitute teacher than to teach an absent teacher's class herself. Running two schools and a parent education program and doing a substantial bit of blind advocacy on the side means that she never sits still for a moment—just the way McQuillan wants her life to be.

THREE TIPS FOR SUCCESS

1. Take the initiative to do what you want to do.
2. If setting up a school is your goal, be sure you enjoy children. As McQuillan puts it, "I always thoroughly enjoyed working with the children, being in their company."
3. Make yourself indispensable. McQuillan says, "I never hesitated to volunteer to work, to take another's shift, to stay late, to come in early." Do whatever it takes to convince your employer [or benefactor] that you are qualified to do the job and be in control.

ADAPTIVE EQUIPMENT: A closed-circuit television, a Type 'n Speak note taker by Blazie Engineering, and a Pentium computer with ZoomText Xtra for screen magnification and speech output. (See the Resources section at the end of this book.)

TOOLS OF THE TRADE: Microsoft Word for writing, Excel for keeping attendance and other records, storytelling skills, and six-string steel acoustic guitar.

SALARY: About $26,000 annually. Benefits include flexibility in scheduling time off and economic benefits in the future because the school property was purchased under a limited liability corporation.

ABOUT RICHARD OEHM

BUSINESS
Oehm Electronics

LOCATION
San Jose, California

AGE
42

CAUSE OF VISUAL IMPAIRMENT
Scarred retinas at birth

VISUAL ACUITY
"I can tell whether the lights are on or off
without listening for the click of a switch."

MANUFACTURER OF TELEVISION AND RADIO TELECOMMUNICATIONS EQUIPMENT

Richard Oehm

"I love being in business for myself."

RICHARD OEHM TALKS ABOUT the world of television and radio signals, cable channels, and bandwidths as though he could see what no one can: the signals zooming through the air that bring pictures and sound into our homes and businesses. As a manufacturer of equipment and a troubleshooter for cable television and the broadcast industry, he discusses radio frequencies and "moving one batch of channels to different channels" with the ease with which others might speak of rearranging office furniture.

After earning his engineering degree from Polytechnical Institute, University of California, and a first-class radio telephone license, Oehm worked for a year or so at TeleSensory Corporation, a company that manufactured access technology. He then moved to a job with Catel. After 14 years with Catel, a former manufacturer of cable equipment, Oehm had become a one-person repair department. The company was floundering, he says, and rather than lay him off, the administrators put him in a position in which they assumed he would fail. He was overloaded with work and frustrated by the additional difficulties posed by blindness.

Files became impossible, unmanageable, and the paperwork voluminous. The company was laying off staff. To cope with the workload, Oehm hired a lot of readers and worked 15-hour days. Since he had no training in computers and needed to learn how to use them, he subscribed to *TACTIC* magazine, a braille and large-print publication on access technology, teaching himself about speech synthesizers and screen access for computer users who are blind. "When I got a computer with the ASAP screen reader and DoubleTalk speech synthesizer," he says, "my 15-hour days went down to 12, and I could sometimes take Sundays and maybe even Saturdays off."

Eventually, however, there were no funds to pay his salary, and his job at Catel ended. Before the company actually went out of business, however, it inadvertently helped Oehm discover a new path. Unable to field customers' cable-related questions or satisfy customers' needs for repair, the remaining Catel employees directed customer after customer to Oehm. "They weren't particularly doing me a favor," he explains. "They just had customers calling and no one to help them. People needed repairs, and Catel would suggest that they call me."

As he puts it, he was looking for a job while he was loaded down with work. One morning in 1993, when he was dressing for a job interview and three companies telephoned begging for his help, he thought of a new possibility: to start his own business. The business of solving problems with cable equipment was already on his doorstep; all he needed to do was focus on accepting it.

Although the business initially concentrated on service—troubleshooting problems with existing equipment—it is moving increasingly toward manufacturing and sales. Oehm builds and sells controllers, boxes, and switches for sending coaxial or fiberoptic signals or for converting one to the other. His customers are radio stations and television stations, both cable and network. Today, he sells equipment to that former boss who let him go, and he has a database of 5,000 other customers as well.

"You don't have to use our controller to use our switches," Oehm explains, "but many companies do. The Oehm Electronics controller is completely interactive. Maybe a channel is getting a snowy picture," he cites as example, "and they have an alternate feed for that same picture. They can tell the system to turn one feed off and the other one on. Or maybe they want to carry a sports event on a particular channel—some are carried nationally and some regionally—so they will call up our box and tell it to switch from the national feed to a regional one." All this communication is conducted electronically. Companies can either use a touch-tone phone to dial Oehm's controller and make necessary changes or send data electronically through a link.

Originally, Oehm worked from his home, where he had converted a two-car garage into a shop area for building equipment. A year after he started the business, however, he got married. Since his wife owned a house as well, the couple decided to live in one and use the other for business. Although 10-hour days are still the norm, Oehm says, the solution has enabled him to put more solid boundaries on his time, leaving work physically and figuratively behind at the end of a day.

It is easy to imagine how this high-energy, fast-talking entrepreneur might have difficulty leaving work alone. Although he now has six employees, he is involved in every aspect of his company. Typically, he devotes most Tuesdays and Thursdays to office and administrative work. He takes orders, prepares and sends all invoices, fine-tunes orders by telephoning a company's technician or engineer to get exact specifications, and plans how to pay for the next batch of parts. The other three days of the week, Oehm makes it a point to go to the shop. Although he has a full-time employee there, he considers it an essential part of his job to "interface" with all work that goes out—and, of course, there are always questions that he has to answer himself. Even on these days, there are telephones to answer, orders to take, faxes to send, and equipment to ship. Oehm has a hand in every detail.

Early in his career, Oehm's avocation as an audiophile led him to market some products specifically for use by broadcasters and recording hobbyists who were blind. "Someone would be calling around, trying to find a way to get, say, an audio readout on a VU meter, and somebody would say, 'Oh, Richard Oehm has something like that.' Word just got around." For years, he has been known among blind engineers and technicians as the source for the audio VU indicator, a device that translates visual information to an audio format to maintain recording levels on broadcast control boards and tape recordings. The device was designed by Smith-Kettlewell Eye Research Institute, which asked Oehm to produce and market the device as a service to the blind community. Oehm refined the original design and has sold 10 to 12 devices a year since 1985.

Other types of adapted audio equipment that he both uses and sells to blind customers include the audio oscilloscope (a device that displays an electrical signal on a CRT screen, allowing the user to see changing voltage over time), talking multimeters, and frequency counters. Although the market for such tools is small, Oehm continues to make them available to blind customers who would otherwise be unable to find them.

The adaptive equipment that Oehm has probably relied most heavily on over the years is the Optacon. Since the 1970s, this device, which converts visual images seen through a lens guided with one hand to tactile images "read" by the other hand, has made it possible for him to "see" essential details in his work that would otherwise be inaccessible. In addition to such routine tasks as sorting mail and looking at catalogs, Oehm has used the Optacon to read schematics and even meters when only visual output was available. "There is simply no other way to actually see what a schematic drawing looks like if you're blind," he says.

Another piece of adaptive equipment that he uses constantly is the Braille 'n Speak notetaker, with which he takes orders, makes notes of telephone conversations, and keeps a small version of his customer database. He puts information on a new customer into the Braille 'n Speak first and later transfers it to the permanent database.

His self-teaching in the 1980s apparently paid off. Oehm now uses computers, equipped with speech and screen access, to do all the paperwork for his business. He generates invoices and quotes; maintains records; and, with the Arkenstone reading system, reads most of his incoming mail.

"I love being in business for myself," he reflects. "I get to do what I like and have opportunities to do things that I probably wouldn't otherwise. The hours are long and demanding if you want to succeed, but the results are great."

THREE TIPS FOR SUCCESS
1. Be sure there are customers for the product or service you intend to provide and know who these customers are.

2. If you are blind, your job takes three to four times the amount of time and effort as it does for sighted people. Be sure you are willing to spend that time and effort.
3. Satisfy the customer. Follow up, double check, and do whatever else it takes to be sure that customers have been given what they want.

ADAPTIVE EQUIPMENT: An Optacon; a Braille 'n Speak notetaker by Blazie Engineering; a Pentium computer with a Window-Eyes screen reader by GW Micro and a DECtalk speech synthesizer by SMART Modular Technologies; Database IV for accounting, invoicing, and other record-keeping; talking multimeters, a talking oscilloscope, and other audio equipment. (See the Resources section at the end of this book.)

SALARY: In 1999, the gross receipts for the business totaled about $300,000, of which Oehm took about $50,000 in salary. As he noted, "Things are in such a state of flux in this business that I'm reluctant to take any more as salary than I absolutely need until I see which way the wind blows."

ABOUT CARMELA CANTISANI

BUSINESS
Carmela's Gourmet

LOCATION
Monterey, California

AGE
48

CAUSE OF VISUAL IMPAIRMENT
Retinitis pigmentosa

VISUAL ACUITY
Light perception

PRODUCER OF GOURMET SALAD DRESSING
Carmela Cantisani

"I work hard because there is competition—the same as everybody else."

W HEN THE CANTISANI FAMILY moved to America from Italy, Carmela Cantisani was 14 years old, and she and her two brothers were sent to boarding schools so they would learn to speak English fluently. Later, Cantisani earned a degree in French from the Monterey Institute of International Studies, studied for a year in France, and traveled to Europe many times. Today, she retains a musical trace of an Italian accent mixed with French, which probably does not hurt business when she does store demonstrations for her gourmet salad dressings.

Although she has always loved to cook, it would be many years before Cantisani turned that passion into a business. As a teacher for the Defense Language Institute, she taught many military personnel to speak conversational Italian comfortably before they left for their overseas assignments. It was intense teaching and, she says, subject to the sorts of subtle discrimination that other blind people have experienced. "Other teachers who couldn't teach worth

103

a darn would be promoted," she recalls, "whereas it was taken for granted that I couldn't do certain things just because I was blind."

Friends and family members had long praised her cooking, particularly her salad dressings, so in 1993, Cantisani decided to turn that creativity into a money-making venture. At first, she made large batches, bottled them in her own kitchen, and sold them to individuals and stores. She and her partner in life and business, Gilbert Converset, registered the name, did some test marketing, and officially launched Carmela's Gourmet. She has been working hard and happily ever since.

The first commercial production was done in 1995 by Esco Foods in San Francisco. "When you have to make thousands of cases of this stuff," she laughs, "you can't do it in your own kitchen anymore. You give your recipes to a plant; they sign an agreement of nondisclosure and manufacture the product for you."

Her six salad dressings are now sold in upscale gourmet and specialty food shops throughout California and other states, with new customers coming on board all the time. The company grew from $1,000 in sales in 1993 to $80,000 in 1998 and is expanding steadily.

The first salad dressing was her original French vinaigrette, called French Authentique because "it's the way they make it in France." In rapid succession, she added Balsamic Vinaigrette with Italian Herbs, Low Fat Provençal (made with herbs from Provence),

Roasted Garlic, Low Fat Caesar, and Mediterranean Mystique. She makes a line of low-fat dressings, she says, because "they are very healthy, and they taste good." Unlike other low-fat products, her products, she maintains, hers have both full-bodied flavor and a low fat count because she purees the vegetables and does not simply add thickeners. Sales indicate that she is right.

Her customer base of about 150 stores, chains, and wholesalers includes Andronico's in northern California and Gelson's in southern California. Cases are also shipped regularly to gourmet and specialty shops in several other states.

Confident that her product is exceptional, Cantisani says that the only hard work is the steady pace required in marketing. She attends two trade shows annually (the Fancy Food Shows in New York and San Francisco) and does numerous food demonstrations in stores up and down the Pacific Coast. For the food demonstrations, she and Converset set up a table with cups of salad dressing and either mixed greens or grilled meat for dipping. "Store demonstrations are the best advertising we could do," Cantisani says. "Once people taste my dressings, the products sell themselves."

The labels of the bottles of salad dressing are as unusual as the contents. Cantisani is proud that hers are the first (and probably only) American food products with braille labels. Producing those labels, however, was a nightmare. First, she brailled them by hand, placing label after label from the preprinted roll into her braille slate and punching the characters with a stylus. A roll of 2,000 labels would take days to braille, and then the huge roll would have to be rewound by hand. Each label needed to be lined up properly by a sighted person, so she could not even finish the task alone.

Next, she tried to subcontract the labeling, but had difficulty finding someone able to do the work. After much persistence, she found someone able to make the plates for brailling that could then be used by a conventional producer of print labels. Today, the labels are produced entirely by Old American Label in Oakland, California.

Although she says the quest was a nightmare, Cantisani was determined not to give up until braille could satisfactorily be placed on every label. She wanted it for others, as well as for herself. "I don't want to have a dinner party with my salad dressing on the table and not know which one is which," she says. "That would be the ultimate insult!"

Although there is substantially more information in print than in braille on each bottle, a braille reader can at least identify the salad dressing by name and read Cantisani's toll-free telephone number. Many people have called, she says, just to comment on how good it is to see the braille—even if they are not braille readers themselves.

Also featured on the label is a picture of Carmela hugging her German shepherd dog guide, Heinz. "He competes with me," she quips; "I sell salad dressings and he sells ketchup." (Actually, dogs are named long before they are matched with their human partners, so the name Heinz was a coincidence.)

Rather than a liability, the tools of blindness are real assets to Cantisani's business. When she conducts store demonstrations, customers frequently stop first because they have noticed her dog guide. "They'll say, 'Oh, the dog! The braille! That's neat!'" she laughs—and then they taste her delicious dressings.

Although Cantisani had recently acquired a laptop with braille display at the time of writing, her methods of keeping information have been simple ones since she established the business. She uses a braille slate and stylus and maintains multiple Rolodex files, filled with 3-by-5-inch cards containing her customers' names and addresses in braille. "I'm so glad I'm a good braille user," she says; "it never fails me, doesn't crash like a computer!"

She and Converset are a good team in business, she believes. She is the creative one who develops the recipes and the extrovert who mingles with the public, whereas he is the one with business sense and accounting skills and the keeper of records.

"In this business," she says, "there is no discrimination because of blindness. I work hard because there is competition—the same as everybody else."

THREE TIPS FOR SUCCESS
1. It is good to have a partner. When times get rough, anxiety does not hit both people the same way or at the same time, so one can move forward with the business.

2. It is important to be realistic. In the beginning, there is a tendency to look ahead, as Cantisani puts it, "counting our money before we got it, dreaming of the mansion and where you want the pool. ... It takes at least three times longer than you think it will take. No matter how good your idea or product, it is hard to get it out there."
3. Be careful of people who promise you the world for a fee. Cantisani recalls, "I lost $13,000 to a company [that] would launch us instantly. ... I know now I can promote the product myself. If the *New York Times* wants to write about me, they will."

ADAPTIVE EQUIPMENT: Eventually, Cantisani plans to use her laptop with an Alva braille display (see the Resources section at the end of this book). So far, however, her primary tools for tracking information have been a braille slate and stylus and Rolodex files.

TOOLS OF THE TRADE: Creativity and good kitchen equipment.

SALARY: The company's sales were $80,000 in 1999, but all profits go back into the company. Cantisani supplements her income with private tutoring and freelance work for the Defense Language Institute.

ABOUT KEVIN KELLEY

BUSINESS
Foresight Engineering

LOCATION
Indianapolis, Indiana

AGE
48

CAUSE OF VISUAL IMPAIRMENT
Port wine birthmark

VISUAL ACUITY
20/500 (6/300, its metric equivalent) in one eye

ENVIRONMENTAL ENGINEER
Kevin Kelley

"I have always felt that I am very fortunate and understood early that it's more important to have what you need than what you want."

K EVIN KELLEY DISPLAYS a brand of spiritual peace and comfortable wisdom that characterise a man decades older. At 48, he views his successful environmental engineering business as more of a hobby than a job, secure in the knowledge that he has created a winner and content to occupy himself with myriad diverse interests. Yet, the business was once his passion, and as much as he attributes its success to good luck and blessings, Kelley clearly has scientific talent and business savvy equal to his knack for growing prize-winning roses.

As a first grader at the Holy Spirit Catholic School in Indianapolis, Kelley was accused of peeking when he covered only one eye. "I was an angelic kid," he says, so reprimands for disobedience were out of character. Once the school received a telephone call from Kelley's parents explaining his visual impairment, "I was called to Sister Superior's office and given an apology."

Being blind in one eye since birth has posed its share of difficulties, but Kelley says that as a child, his real limitation was the birthmark that he would one day learn to be the probable cause for his visual impairment. Having a visible physical difference was sometimes a painful barrier to socializing, he says, and occasionally poses difficulties even today. But Kelley has made it his life's focus to recognize limitations as well as assets and to make the best of both.

With 20/20 vision in one eye and none in the other, Kelley was able to use regular print with a magnifying glass through his second year of college. It was then that he realized that his remaining eye had severe problems, too. The birthmark, which spreads from the eyes to the upper lip, had spread behind the retina and lifted it off the eye. His rapidly diminishing vision inspired him to change the direction of his career.

His initial choice had been to be a veterinarian, but discouraged by the fact that he could not see enough detail to satisfy laboratory assignments in preveterinary courses, he changed his major. "The Environmental Protection Agency was just getting started," he explains, "and Purdue had begun a program called Natural Resources and Environmental Science. The advantage was that there was no foreign language requirement, which there was in engineering, so I changed my major." In 1974, Kelley graduated from Purdue University with a degree in environmental science.

"Moses was really the first waste-water operator," he says. "Somewhere in Mosaic law, there must be a line that says something like, "Thou shalt go into the desert and thou shalt take a shovel!'"

The environmental engineering field was just becoming serious business in the United States in the early 1970s, and Kelley was ready for it. For several years, he was the primary design engineer of waste-water projects for one of the largest environmental engineering firms in Indiana. In 1989, he resigned. "I have always felt that I am very fortunate and understood early that it's more important to have what you need than what you want," Kelley says. "Fairness and integrity have always been of uppermost importance to me, in business and personal life, and I felt that money was gaining primary importance in that company. . . . When I turned in my resignation, I had no idea what I was going to do next."

He bought his own computer system, equipped with magnification and speech, and eventually started his own environmental engineering business. His first employer, now his best friend, gave him an enormous boost when he handed over several clients. Smaller towns and municipalities throughout Indiana constitute his primary customer base. Foresight Engineering provides planning, design, construction management, and support services for towns, cities, institutions, and private developers related to the control of water pollution and to the supply, treatment, storage, and drainage of water with environmentally sound techniques. Sometimes the company does landscaping and recommends plantings for municipalities and businesses. Over the years, Kelley has been involved with every aspect of that work, but his goal is eventually to provide more support than leadership.

Today, with eight employees, Kelley no longer does design work himself. His job, he says, is much more fun: He writes letters, meets with clients to solve problems, handles numerous telephone calls, and makes suggestions for others' designs. "I get to pass out paychecks and eat doughnuts," he laughs.

In 1998, his chief design engineer bought into the business and is now the co-owner. That bit of progress suits Kelley's goals just fine. "To whom much is given, much is required," he says. "I have created a successful business. I own my own home. I have everything I want. It's time to begin giving back."

Kelley landscapes his own property (including the planting of some two dozen trees and building a 10-by-15-foot pool with a 5-foot waterfall), and has become a master rose gardener and a collector of autographed baseballs. In addition to developing such avocations, however, his goal is to volunteer more extensively—possibly in a disability ministry with his church or with Canine Companions for Independence. At this point, however, his "hobby" of running a company still claims the majority of his time.

He uses several closed-circuit television (CCTV) systems, as well as human readers, at home and at work to see print. His 25-year habit of handwriting

114

rough drafts is still the norm, which he says his secretary and others manage to decipher for the preparation of final documents. "The beauty of owning my own company," he says, "is that I can have others assist me with the tasks I have to do."

Until late 1999, when the expansion of the company necessitated moving the office to larger quarters 2½ miles away, Kelley walked the one mile from his home to his office. His solution was to hire his mother, now 79, to drive him to and from work. "When she's not available, someone else gives me a ride or I take a cab," he says, "but we're getting a big kick out of saying we've hired a senior citizen. She says she probably makes more now at $40 a week for driving me than she did on her last job as an office manager in the late 1940s."

With ZoomText Xtra on his computer, as well as Window-Eyes for reading larger text files, Kelley uses his computer extensively on the job. Much of the business is maintaining contacts, he says, and he uses a contact management program called ACT! to track some 450 names and addresses. "With Zoom-Text Xtra," he explains, "I can look up a contact I need to call, click on the phone number, and the computer dials it for me. If I need to read it to someone else, I can do that as well."

Busy but content would be an apt description for Kelley, who is active in his profession, his church, and his community. When the company needs him less, he has a laundry list of volunteer pursuits and avocations he would like to pursue. Meanwhile, he has no difficulty making time, when whim necessitates, to tend his roses or immerse himself in baseball's spring training. "I see part of my job as running the company and part of my job as helping others in whatever way I can," he says simply. According to Kelley's personal creed, that is just what you do with a lifetime of blessings.

THREE TIPS FOR SUCCESS
1. Recognize and admit to your limitations.
2. Look for ways in which you can take your limitations, perceived as disadvantages, and turn them into advantages.
3. If you plan to add staff, look to surround yourself with people whose abilities complement yours and with whom, working as a team, you find a balance of covering for one another's limitations to maximize the positive.

ADAPTIVE EQUIPMENT: Several CCTVs for reading print materials; a computer equipped with Zoom-Text Xtra by Ai Squared for screen magnification and speech output; a Window-Eyes screen reader by GW Micro and a DECtalk synthesizer by SMART Modular Technologies for reading larger files; an assortment of handheld magnifiers (which are of limited use with diminishing vision); and Dragon Dictate, which Kelley is "beginning to learn to use" for speech input. (See the Resources section at the end of this book.)

TOOLS OF THE TRADE: Contact-management software called ACT! for maintaining a database of contacts and clients.

SALARY: Kelley draws only $12,000 annually because that is all he needs. His partner, however, draws $60,000 to $80,000, which he projects is reasonable for running a similar company.

ABOUT CRISTA EARL

BUSINESS
CrissCross Technologies

LOCATION
Forest Hills, New York

AGE
42

CAUSE OF VISUAL IMPAIRMENT
Macular degeneration

VISUAL ACUITY
Peripheral vision only.

CREATOR OF AUDIO COMPUTER TUTORIALS

Crista Earl

"This is absolutely the most fun I've ever had."

SPANISH WAS THE LANGUAGE Crista Earl was pursuing when she enrolled as a freshman at Indiana University. It had been her primary subject in high school and would be her major in college. In her second semester, however, she was introduced to another language that would eventually dominate her work life: the language of computers.

A talking word-processing program called Documents was donated to the engineering department's Apple Lab, and though it was primitive by today's standards, Earl remembers being thrilled with it. "It was way better than a typewriter for writing all my papers," she says, and she was hooked.

She began studying AppleSoft Basic and eventually took most of the computer courses the university had to offer. At the time, the university did not offer a major in computers or programming, but Earl estimates that she took far more courses than would have constituted a minor.

She began to learn about personal computers (PCs), too, and finally bought her first computer, a 128K PC JR. "This was 1983 or 1984," she explains, "when everyone was struggling over whether to go with Apple or with PC. For no good reason, I picked the right one." Earl wrote her own programs in BASIC to make the first computer read the screen aloud and shudders now to think how laborious it was. She was working part time for her father, who owned a nuts-and-bolts business, and had the entire 10,000-piece inventory stored on the floppy disks for that computer. "There was no way to stop it," she says, laughing. "If you started out in the wrong menu, you just had to hear the whole thing."

Earl's vision problem was diagnosed as macular degeneration when she was a third grader in her Fort Wayne, Indiana, public school. By the fourth grade, she could no longer read regular print. With a collection of special lenses and telescoping glasses, she read large print through high school, but by the time she entered college, she could see only the format of a page and was no longer able to read it. In high school, she began to use an increasing number of books on audiotape and by college, she had developed a comfortable balance between audiotapes and live readers.

Tutoring in both Spanish and computers throughout college sometimes provided built-in readers for her. Her students would read a problem from the book, she recalls, and she would, in turn, help them work out the computer code.

In 1987, she was offered a job with Computer Aids Corporation, a now-defunct Fort Wayne-based company specializing in talking computer products. "They handed me a real PC with a real screen reader," she recalls, "and I was kicking myself for not knowing about these things sooner." In 1992, she began working in technical support for GW Micro, the company that distributes Vocal-Eyes and Window-Eyes screen readers for people who are blind and visually impaired. What she enjoyed most was one-on-one training, providing people with the help they needed to use powerful computing tools. Transportation in Fort Wayne was terrible, however, and getting to the people who needed her help was always difficult. When she came to New York City in 1996, she knew that she was finally going to begin her own business.

From a business standpoint, she had done enough things wrong while in Fort Wayne to know how to do them right when she moved to New York. She immediately opened a business checking account; gave her company a name, CrissCross Technologies; designed a logo; and began advertising.

People knew her name and reputation from her work at GW Micro, so getting clients was never difficult. "But there were so many people who needed help," she recalls, "and I could get to only so many of them. Doug Wakefield had once done some great things on tape, but now there was a huge void. I had kicked around the idea of making tutorials for a long time, but didn't know how to get going with the recording stuff. I decided to begin figuring it out [and] to make at least one tutorial to get more people over the hump."

In addressing these problems, Earl maintains that New York is the best place in the world to be. There are many people with answers to questions, particularly audio-related questions. "You can't go half a block without finding three audio stores," she says, "and at least one of them is going to have the answer you need."

Speaking of Windows 3.X, her first product, consisted of two audiocassettes, packaged in a cassette album with braille and print labels. As with all her tutorials, listeners hear Earl's voice progressing step by step through basic how-to lessons. They also hear "Harry," the voice of the DECtalk speech synthesizer, responding to commands and reading the screen as it will for blind customers who follow the tutorial's instructions.

Speaking of Windows 3.X sold for $60, and every time Earl sold 10 more, she thought that might be the end of it. But customers kept ordering more copies and asking for more titles. At this point, there are nine in all—including *Speaking of the Internet, Speaking of Excel, Speaking of Microsoft Word,* and upgraded versions of *Speaking of Windows.*

Listening to Earl's chatty, informal manner on the tapes makes the whole business of CrissCross Technologies sound deceptively easy. Actually, the process of producing the tutorials is extremely complex. "At first, I couldn't stand the sound of my own voice," she recalls. Then, there was the problem of "me being way soft and Harry being way loud."

Today, she records on a professional four-track recorder, plugs the recorder into the computer's sound card, and uses a program designed for editing sound to set levels and edit and time segments. By recording the various segments of a tutorial in any order she pleases, she can then add them up and rearrange them so that each side of a tape lasts exactly 41 minutes.

In 1997, she went to work part time for the American Foundation for the Blind as a resource specialist and needed to hire assistants to keep CrissCross Technologies going. Today, she has three part-time employees who manage the business while she works full time at AFB as a national technology associate. Beyond her hours at AFB, her time—and space—are consumed by her own business. "The large living room and entryway of my apartment are completely taken over by CrissCross Technologies," she says. Both areas are lined with shelves, filing cabinets, and equipment. Even in the bedroom, everything above eye level is CrissCross Technologies' products.

Although such crowded quarters might sound daunting to some, Earl would not have it any other way. "This is absolutely the most fun I've ever had," she maintains. She is always planning ahead for new tutorials and, in January 1999, launched an ongoing series of minitutorials for advanced computer users. *Listening In,* a single tape focusing on a particular topic, is issued bimonthly.

Two of her three employees are blind, and Earl is proud that the entire operation is "blind friendly." Everything is labeled in braille. The entire database of inventory, invoices, accounts payable, and other

123

types of records is recorded in Excel and is easily accessed with a screen reader. Her sighted employee learned the braille numbers 1–10, and it is her job to label all incoming invoices and receipts and enter them in Excel so that anyone at CrissCross can retrieve them easily. "It took me years to figure out my system for organizing those things," Earl explains, "but it works really well."

Earl was a late bloomer when it came to learning braille, but now she finds it hard to imagine functioning without it. She taught herself when she was in her 30s, and though she still would not read a novel in braille, she finds braille to be the most efficient way of keeping notes and labeling files.

A Mailboxes Etc. store down the block is her point of shipping and receiving, so that no shipments or orders come to her apartment. "When I have orders to go out," she says, "I just load up my cart and take it down there, and they do all the shipping for me. I love it."

With a database of 4,000 customers, many of whom are dealers, Earl is clearly not the only one who loves what CrissCross Technologies is doing.

THREE TIPS FOR SUCCESS
1. Hire help. There are things you cannot or should not do. For example, if it is going to take four hours to get somewhere with public transportation but 30 minutes by car, hire a driver. Your time is an important part of your business.

2. Develop a great filing system. As Earl found, "When I had a problem with an American Express bill, I could pull it out of a file folder for review."
3. Do not be afraid to put your money back into your business. Purchasing additional equipment is money well spent because it helps you use your time more effectively.

ADAPTIVE EQUIPMENT: A Dell Pentium 450 computer, with 128MB RAM; Window-Eyes and Vocal-Eyes screen readers by GW Micro; a DECtalk PC speech synthesizer by SMART Modular Technologies; a Home Page Reader Web browser by IBM Accessibility Center; Open Book Unbound and Open Book Ruby PC-based optical character recognition systems by Arkenstone; a Braille Lite 2000 notetaker and Braille Blazer printer by Blazie Engineering; and a Juliet printer by Enabling Technologies. (See the Resources section at the end of this book.)

TOOLS OF THE TRADE: Two Tascam professional recorders; a Tascam dual tape deck for editing and making masters; a SoundForge program for editing sound files; a CD burner for storing tutorial tracks on CDs; two high-speed tape duplicators that each make three cassette copies at a time; Excel; WordPerfect 8.0 for Windows for making brochures, labels, invoices, and the like; and an inkjet printer.

SALARY: Gross sales were $75,000 in 1999.

GEORGE WURTZEL

BUSINESS
Kitchen Encounter

LOCATION
Lansing, Michigan

AGE
45

CAUSE OF VISUAL IMPAIRMENT
Retinitis pigmentosa

VISUAL ACUITY
"In winter, I can tell that the sun is shining."

WOODWORKER AND CABINETMAKER
George Wurtzel

"I have always been convinced that if there was something I wanted to do, I could find a way to learn to do it."

G EORGE WURTZEL ENJOYS surprising people. Once, a bank executive came looking for "the blind guy" he had heard was working on the teller-line installation project. "He's up there," Wurtzel's assistant responded, pointing to the big man climbing easily around the scaffolding overhead. The banker was stunned, and the job was a huge success. Wurtzel smiles as he tells the story, knowing that his part in the tale contradicted every common stereotype of what a "blind guy" can do. That is all right with him: His business sense tells him that if people remember him, they will come back for more business.

For over 20 years, Wurtzel has made his mark as a woodworker, cabinetmaker, and furniture builder throughout Michigan and elsewhere. Much of the work he has done with the easy poise that is common in confident artists, but no matter how much he loves his work, he is clearly in it for business.

As a student at the Michigan State School for the Blind and at Traverse City High School, Wurtzel studied woodworking and auto mechanics. His first job was as a mechanic for a Volkswagen dealer.

Later, while Wurtzel was working as a bicycle mechanic in Traverse City, his employer mentioned that the shop needed showcases, and he recalls blurting impulsively, "I'll do that." He had never built anything and was not sure how to do so, but the challenge was irresistible. With tools and work space lent by a friend, the cases were completed.

Wurtzel began to spend more and more time in his friend's woodworking shop. Eventually, he assisted a friend in building boats and then lawn chairs, and by 1974, he had bought his own table saw, radial arm saw, joiner (for making the edges of boards smooth), and an assortment of hand tools.

By trading building maintenance and snow shoveling for rent, Wurtzel set up shop in the basement of a commercial office building and established himself as an architectural mill woodworker. "Anything that goes into a building, we build," he explains, citing such examples as bars, cash register counters, dental labs, gift-wrapping counters, and clothing displays. Restaurants and bars were major customers with all the cabinets, shelves, and spaces for appliances that needed customized woodwork for support.

"It was the easiest work to find," Wurtzel says. "Traverse City is a resort town, and bars were always changing hands." With the remodeling by new owners would come new specifications for refrigeration units, drink machines, ice makers, dishwashers, and cabinets—and Wurtzel would construct the counters and cabinets accordingly.

In the late 1970s, Wurtzel had eight or nine employees working for him, but the economic conditions in Michigan changed dramatically. In 1982, with a 25 percent unemployment rate statewide, Wurtzel closed his business and headed for North Carolina to go back to college. He enrolled at Catawba Valley College in Hickory, North Carolina, to obtain an associate degree in furniture production management.

When he showed up for class, Wurtzel recalls, the school administrators were astonished. "They had no clue that I was blind, and initially, they freaked out," he laughs. He showed his portfolio, explained what he could do, and began attending classes.

After he obtained his degree, Wurtzel went to work for a furniture sample builder, making the design samples used in showrooms and furniture stores. He built occasional tables, coffee tables, chairs, and frames for couches and settees—every sort of furniture in a range of styles from traditional to Scandinavian to wildly contemporary. Although he loved the work, he eventually realized that he preferred to be in business for himself and returned to Michigan to start a new company.

In 1997, Wurtzel, together with two partners, two salespeople, and two woodworkers, opened Kitchen

Encounter. Located in the historic district of Lansing, Michigan, this 4,000-square-foot retail store boasts 13 kitchen displays and a wide range of choices for renovating, remodeling, fabricating, and installing kitchen counters and cabinets; another 4,000-square-foot building across the alley serves as workshop and fabrication facility.

As president of the company, Wurtzel does a bit of everything; he prepares bids, solicits business, installs kitchens, and checks the work of all his employees.

He has used few adaptations to do woodworking over the years but adapts his own techniques as a blind person to use existing tools. For measurements, for instance, he has always used a click rule—a telescoping measuring device with 16 threads to the inch—and says that his employees all believe his measurements are consistently more accurate than anyone else's. Whereas a sighted cabinetmaker might draw a pencil line as a cutting guide, Wurtzel fastens a wood block or other tactile indicator. His style has always been to use a little ingenuity to develop an adaptation when the ordinary method demands sight.

He relishes the hands-on labor of tearing out old kitchens and installing new ones and is always amused by the element of surprise his blindness initially stirs in customers. "I met an electrical inspector on the job," he smiles, "and he said, 'Oh, I heard there was a blind guy with a builder's license! How do you do that?'" Wurtzel's characteristic reply was, "Very well, thank you."

His innate sense of space and direction have served him in other ways, too. He uses a white cane when he takes the bus or walks the three miles to work, although he has never had a formal mobility lesson. "I get where I want to go, so my skills must be adequate," he jokes.

Wurtzel has a sense of humor and a relaxed attitude toward his blindness, but he also recognizes the advantages it brings to business. When customers realize that there is a blind craftsman on the job, their curiosity is piqued; then their satisfaction is perhaps even greater because of the element of awe. Wurtzel also demonstrates his entrepreneurial savvy in seeking business in areas where minority contractors are given priority, realizing that his disability gives his company "minority business" status.

Although his building and woodworking skills are outstanding, Wurtzel is always adding credentials to his repertoire to position himself better as a business owner. Since he established Kitchen Encounter, he has attended classes in kitchen design at the local community college, gone to a school in Minnesota that specializes in the fabrication of solid surface countertops, become the first blind person in his state to earn a builder's license, and attended a Chicago seminar conducted by Dupont Corian to become a certified Corian technician. (Corian is a countertop surface used frequently in restaurants, and special techniques are required for fabricating and installing it.)

To keep itemized lists of parts and to prepare price quotes, Wurtzel uses a Braille 'n Speak, Braille Blaz-

131

er, and ink jet printer. Although his vision enabled him to read large print in his student days at the Michigan State School for the Blind, all children in those days were taught to read and write braille as well. Wurtzel credits those lessons with much of his success today.

All work orders and other documentation at his store are provided to him on floppy disks in ASCII format that he then loads into his Braille 'n Speak for review. "If you're the president of the company," he says, "you have a little influence in the way things are done. . . . Print information is always accessible to me because that's just the way they're used to doing things."

Wurtzel purchased a house that needs a complete renovation and has nearly finished remodeling it himself in his spare time. There is nothing in terms of electrical wiring, carpentry, or repair that he has not tried, he says, and he loves it all. His favorite part of woodworking? "People think I'm strange," he says, "but what I love best is the finishing, tending to all of those fine details at the end of a project. You can have a beautiful piece of furniture or woodwork, but if it isn't finished properly, the beauty can be lost."

THREE TIPS FOR SUCCESS

1. "The Braille 'n Speak has just been magic," Wurtzel notes. "It is such a tremendous advantage to be able to pick up such an incredible amount of information and carry it around."

2. Learn to read and write braille. Wurtzel was taught to use braille in the third grade, even though he was still able to read large-print books. Today, he maintains that he could not possibly do the work he does without braille literacy. "I can't imagine how you could take down cutting lists and mark things off without braille," he says.
3. Have self-confidence. As Wurtzel puts it, "I have always been convinced that if there was something I wanted to do, I could find a way to learn to do it."

ADAPTIVE EQUIPMENT: A Braille 'n Speak note taker, a Braille Blazer printer, and a disk drive to transfer files to and from the Braille 'n Speak, made by Blazie Engineering; an ink jet printer; and commercially available tools with adaptive qualities, such as a click rule, an electronic level with audio output, and a stud finder with audio output. (See the Resources section at the end of this book.)

TOOLS OF THE TRADE: table saws, routers, planers, joiners, and "the normal gamut of woodworking tools."

SALARY: Wurtzel expects to clear $50,000 in a year's time. The average furniture maker or cabinetmaker earns about $15 an hour.

RESOURCES

Although providing detailed information on starting your own business is beyond the scope of this book, several national organizations for people who are blind or visually impaired have programs related to careers and business ownership. In addition, many organizations and companies disseminate information, distribute adaptive equipment, and provide referrals and other forms of assistance to people who are blind or visually impaired. This section contains a sampling of these resources.

SOURCES OF INFORMATION

National Organizations

The three national organizations listed in this section provide information and referrals, publish books and journals, and serve as advocates for people who are visually impaired. The American Foundation for the Blind's (AFB's) National Technology Center is a resource for information on adaptive technology products, and AFB's Careers and Technology Information Bank is a nationwide database of blind and visually impaired people who mentor others who are seeking advice on careers. The American Council of the Blind and the National Federation of the Blind, membership organizations for people who are blind or visually impaired, each have special-interest groups for visually impaired entrepreneurs.

American Council of the Blind
1155 15th Street, N.W., Suite 720
Washington, DC 20005
Phone: (202) 467-5081 or (800) 424-8666
Fax: (202) 467-5085
E-mail: info@acb.org
URL: www.acb.org
Serves as a representative national membership organization of blind people, with affiliates nationwide. Promotes effective participation of blind people in all aspects of society; provides information and referral, advocacy, consultation, and a job bank; and conducts a public education program to promote greater understanding of blindness and the capabilities of blind people. Publishes the Braille Forum, a free monthly national magazine. The following affiliate may be of interest to people who are thinking of starting their own businesses:

Independent Visually Impaired Enterprisers
Carla Hayes, President
230 Robinhood Lane
McMurray, PA 15317

American Foundation for the Blind
11 Penn Plaza, Suite 300
New York, NY 10001
Phone (212) 502-7600, (212) 502-7662
(TTY/TDD), or (800) AFB-LINE

Fax: (212) 502-7777
E-mail: afbinfo@afb.net
URL: http://www.afb.org
Provides services to and acts as an information clearinghouse for people who are blind or visually impaired and their families, professionals, organizations, schools, and corporations. Operates the National Technology Center and the Career and Technology Information Bank; stimulates research and mounts program initiatives to improve services to blind and visually impaired persons, including the National Initiative on Literacy, the National Technology Program, and the AFB Textbook and Instructional Materials Solutions Forum. Advocates for services and legislation; maintains the M. C. Migel Library and Information Center. Produces videos and publishes books, pamphlets, the *Directory of Services for Blind and Visually Impaired Persons in the United States and Canada,* the *Journal of Visual Impairment & Blindness,* and *AccessWorld: Technology for Consumers with Visual Impairments.*

National Federation of the Blind
1800 Johnson Street
Baltimore, MD 21230
Phone: (410) 659-9314
Fax: (410) 685-5653
E-mail: epc@roudley.com
URL: http://www.nfb.org
As a consumer and advocacy membership organization with affiliates nationwide, strives to improve social and economic conditions of blind persons;

acts as a vehicle for collective self-expression; provides information and referral services, information about adaptive equipment and technology, information about job opportunities, and public education about blindness. Publishes the Braille Monitor. The following divisions may be of interest to people who are thinking of starting their own businesses:

Blind Merchants Association
of the National Federation of the Blind
Don Morris, President
16547 Old Emmitsburg Road
Emmitsburg, Maryland 21727-8927
Phone: (301) 447-6380

National Association of Blind Entrepreneurs
Connie Leblond, President
15 May Street
Portland, Maine 04102-3710
Phone: (207) 772-7305

Small Business and Self-Employment Service
Job Accommodation Network
P.O. Box 6080
Morgantown, WV 26506-6080
Phone: (800) 526-7234 (V/TT)
Fax: (304) 293-5407
E-mail: kcording@wvu.edu
URL: http://www.janweb.icdi.wvu.edu/SBSES
As a service of the President's Committee on Employment of People with Disabilities, provides comprehensive information, counseling, and referrals about self-employment and opportunities to own small businesses for people with disabilities.

PUBLICATIONS AND SOURCES OF BOOKS AND OTHER MATERIALS

The publications and sources of books and other materials that are listed here provide invaluable information in accessible forms.

AccessWorld: Technology for Consumers with Visual Impairments
AccessWorld Subscriptions
The Sheridan Press
450 Fame Avenue
Hanover, PA 17331
Phone: (888) 522-0220 or (717) 632-3535
Fax: (717) 633-8900
URL: http://www.afb.org/accessworld.html
A bimonthly periodical on adaptive technology and visual impairment; successor to TACTIC. Published by the American Foundation for the Blind.

Dialogue
c/o Blindskills
P.O. Box 5181
Salem, OR 97304
Phone: (503) 581-4224 or (800) 860-1224
Fax: (503) 581-0178
E-mail: blindskl@teleport.com
URL: http://www.teleport.com/blindskl
A quarterly general-interest magazine for people who are blind or visually impaired.

Journal of Visual Impairment & Blindness
JVIB Subscriptions
The Sheridan Press
450 Fame Avenue

Hanover, PA 17331
Phone: (888) 522-0220 or (717) 632-3535
Fax: (717) 633-8900
URL: http://www.afb.org/jvib.html
A monthly interdisciplinary journal publishing scholarly articles and serving as a forum for the exchange of ideas on visual impairment and blindness. Includes features on employment and technology. Published by the American Foundation for the Blind.

National Library Service for the Blind and Physically Handicapped
Library of Congress
1291 Taylor Street, N.W.
Washington, DC 20542
Phone: (202) 707-5100 or (800) 424-8567
Fax: (202) 707-0712
E-mail: nls@loc.gov
URL: http://www.loc.gov/nls
Distributes free braille and recorded materials of a general nature to individuals who are blind or visually impaired. Provides reference information on all aspects of visual impairment and other physical disabilities that affect reading.

Recording for the Blind and Dyslexic
20 Roszel Road
Princeton, NJ 08540
Phone: (609) 452-0606 or (800) 221-4792
Fax: (609) 987-8116
E-mail: info@rfbd.org
URL: http://www.rfbd.org
Provides recorded and computerized textbooks, library services, and other educational resources to

people who cannot read standard print. Maintains a lending library of recorded books and acts as a recording service for additional titles.

SOURCES OF ADAPTIVE PRODUCTS AND DEVICES

The following list provides the names of companies and organizations from which adaptive materials and equipment that are mentioned in this book can be obtained.

Advanced Access Devices
2066-C Walsh Avenue
Santa Clara, CA 95050
Phone: (408) 970-9760
Fax: (408) 727-9351
E-mail: info@aagi.com
Web site: http://www.aagi.com
   SuperBraille laptop with braille display.

Ai Squared
P.O. Box 669
Manchester Center, VT 05255
Phone: (802) 362-3612
Fax: (802) 362-1670
E-mail: sales@aisquared.com or
support@aisquared.com
URL: http://www.aisquared.com
   ZoomText Xtra screen magnification software.

Alva Access Group
436 14th Street, Suite 700
Oakland, CA 94612
Phone: (510) 923-6280

Fax: (510) 451-0878
E-mail: info@aagi.com
Web site: http://www.aagi.com/
   OutSPOKEN screen reader.
   Alva refreshable braille display.

American Thermoform Corporation
2311 Travers Avenue
City of Commerce, CA 90040
Phone: (800) 331-3676 or (213) 723-9021
Fax: (213) 728-8877
E-mail: atc@atcbrleqp.com
URL: http://www.atcbrleqp.com
   Braillon labels.

Arkenstone, Inc.
NASA Ames Moffett Complex, Building 23
P.O. Box 215
Moffett Field, CA 94035-0215
Phone: (800) 444-4443 or (650) 603-8880
Fax: (650) 603-8887
E-mail: info@arkenstone.org
URL: http://www.arkenstone.org
   Open Book Unbound and Open Book Ruby
      Edition, PC-based optical character
      recognition systems.

Blazie Engineering
105 East Jarrettsville Road
Forest Hill, MD 21050
Phone: (410) 893-9333
Fax: (410) 836-5040
E-mail: info@blazie.com
URL: http://blazie.com
   Braille Blazer printer.

Braille Lite notetaker.
Braille 'n Speak notetaker.
Type 'n Speak notetaker with computer-style
   keyboard.

Duxbury Systems
270 Littleton Road, Unit 6
Westford, MA 01886-3523
Phone: (978) 692-3000
Fax: (978) 692-7912
E-mail: info@duxsys.com
Web site: http://www.duxburysystems.com
   Duxbury braille translator.
   Megadots braille translator.

Enabling Technologies Company
1601 Northeast Braille Place
Jensen Beach, FL 34957
Phone: (800) 777-3687 or (561) 225-3687
Fax: (561) 225-3299
E-mail: enabling@brailler.com
URL: http://www.brailler.com
   Bookmaker braille printer.
   Express 100 braille printer.
   Index braille printer.
   Juliet braille printer.

GW Micro
725 Airport North Office Park
Fort Wayne, IN 46825
Phone: (219) 489-3671
Fax: (219) 489-2608
E-mail: support@gwmicro.com
URL: http://www.gwmicro.com
   Window-Eyes screen reader.

Henter-Joyce
11800 31st Court North
St. Petersburg, FL 33716
Phone: (800) 336-5658 or (813) 803-8000
Fax: (813) 803-8001
E-mail: info@hj.com
URL: http://www.hj.com
　　JAWS screen reader.

Howe Press of the Perkins School for the Blind
175 North Beacon Street
Watertown, MA 02172
Phone: (617) 924-3490
　　Perkins Brailler.

IBM Accessibility Center
Building 901, Internal Zip 9171
11400 Burnet Road
Austin, TX 78758
Phone: (800) 426-4832 or (512) 838-4598
URL: http://www.ibm.com/sns
　　Home Page Reader Web browser.

MicroTalk Software
3039 Aubert Avenue
Louisville, KY 40206
Phone: (502) 897-5789
Fax: (502) 721-6083
E-mail: larry@microtalk.com
URL: http://www.microtalk.com
　　ASAP screen reader.

RC Systems
1609 England Avenue
Everett, WA 98203
Phone: (206) 355-3800

Fax: (425) 355-1098
E-mail: info@rcsys.com
URL: http://www.rcsys.com
   Double Talk speech synthesizer.

SMART Modular Technologies
4305 Cushing Parkway
Freemont, CA 94538
Phone: (800) 225-5385
E-mail: carl.leeber@smartm.com
URL: http://www.smartmodulartech.com/systems
/products/dectalk/assistive_view/adtsupport.htm/
   DECtalk speech synthesizer

TeleSensory Corporation
520 Almanor Avenue
Sunnyvale, CA 94086-3533
Phone: (800) 286-8484 or (408) 616-8700
Fax: (408) 616-8753
E-mail: info@telesensory.com
URL: http://www.telesensory.com
   Reading AdvantEdge PC-based optical
      character recognition system.
   David laptop with braille display.
   Optacon. (TeleSensory Corporation no longer
      manufactures the Optacon but continues to
      provide service.)

About the Author

Deborah Kendrick, author of the Jobs That Matter series, is an award-winning writer, editor, columnist, and poet. The writer of the column "Alive and Well," which appears weekly in the *Cincinnati Enquirer, Columbus Dispatch*, and other newspapers, she also writes a regular column on family issues for *Dialogue*, a general-interest magazine for adolescents and adults who are blind, and she is contributing editor of *AccessWorld*, a journal on technology for visually impaired consumers. Kendrick has written hundreds of features, editorials, and reviews, many of them on disability-related issues, for *Woman's Day, Parenting, Executive Lifestyles, Marriage and Family*, and many other publications. Author of *Jobs To Be Proud Of: Profiles of Workers Who Are Blind or Visually Impaired*, which was honored with the American Council of the Blind's Vernon Henley Media Award in 1994, she was named a "role model for women" by Women in Communications and was recipient of the American Foundation for the Blind's 1993 Access Award. Her most recent book is *Teachers Who Are Blind or Visually Impaired*.

Kendrick, who has been blind since childhood, has received numerous other honors for her efforts as journalist and advocate, including the 1997 Maurice McCracken Peace and Justice Award and the National Easter Seal Society's 1995 Grand EDI Award for Print Journalism. A former educator in both elementary and graduate-level classrooms, she continues her connection with young people through school presentations and in-service workshops for teachers. She has three children and lives in Cincinnati, Ohio.